# 50

## MATHS LESSONS FOR MORE ABLE LEARNERS

- Age-appropriate lessons to stretch confident learners
- Ideas to accelerate progress through objectives
- Bank of challenging brainteasers

## AGES 5-7

Judy Sayers and
Debbie Morgan

# Credits

**Authors**
Judy Sayers and
Debbie Morgan

**Editors**
Sara Wiegand
Christine Vaughan
Kim Vernon

**Assistant Editor**
Margaret Eaton

**Illustrations**
Gaynor Berry

**Series Designer**
Catherine Perera

**Designer**
Catherine Perera

Text © 2007 Judy Sayers and Debbie Morgan
© 2007 Scholastic Ltd

Designed using Adobe InDesign

Published by Scholastic Ltd
Villiers House
Clarendon Avenue
Leamington Spa
Warwickshire CV32 5PR

www.scholastic.co.uk

Printed by Bell and Bain Ltd, Glasgow.

2 3 4 5 6 7 8 9          9 0 1 2 3 4 5 6

**Mixed Sources**
Product group from well-managed
forests and other controlled sources
www.fsc.org  Cert no. TT-COC-002769
© 1996 Forest Stewardship Council
FSC

**British Library Cataloguing-in-Publication Data**
A catalogue record for this book is available from the British Library.

ISBN 0-439-94527-5
ISBN 978-0439-94527-1

The right of Judy Sayers and Debbie Morgan to be identified as the authors of this work has been asserted by them in accordance with the Copyright, Designs and Patents Act 1988.

Extracts from the Primary National Strategy's *Primary Framework for Mathematics* (2006) www.standards.dfes.gov.uk/primaryframework © Crown copyright. Reproduced under the terms of the Click Use Licence.

510.
7
FIF

# Contents

## About the series

*50 Maths Lessons for More Able Learners* is a series of three books designed for teachers working with higher ability children within the daily mathematics lesson. Each title will address the principles of inclusion for more confident learners identified in *Excellence and Enjoyment: Learning and Teaching in the Primary Years* (DfES, 2004). Each book covers a two-year span of the primary age range: KS1 5-7 and KS2 7-9 and 9-11.

Each title consists of 20 short 'brainteaser' activities and 50 lesson plans, each with an accompanying photocopiable activity page. The activities cover many of the objectives in the Primary National Strategy's revised *Primary Framework for Mathematics* (2006). The lesson plans and accompanying photocopiable activities are designed to:
● set suitable learning challenges for more able learners
● accelerate progress through learning objectives
● provide tasks that are more open-ended or extended in time and complexity
● fit into the individual teacher's existing planning for mathematics.

## How to use this book

This book begins with a detailed Objectives grid, giving an overview of the objectives addressed by each lesson. Teachers can also use this grid to track forward to identify appropriate objectives from later years where necessary.

## Brainteaser activities

A bank of 20 brainteaser activities follows (with linked photocopiable sheets on pages 18-27). The purpose of these activities is to provide short, focused opportunities to stretch more able pupils. Where relevant, links to brainteaser activities are included on the lesson plans. However, they can also be used flexibly as required - for example, you may want to map similar brainteasers with the theme of a lesson, or extend learning as a homework or assessment task.

## Lesson plans

To make the book easy to use, all 50 lesson plans follow the same format:

### Learning objectives

Each lesson is written to address one or more of the PNS strands from Years 1 and 2. Where appropriate, objective links to Year 3 are also included.

### Expected prior knowledge

This incorporates a brief summary of what children should be expected to know or do before starting each lesson.

### Key vocabulary

Key mathematical vocabulary linked to the PNS Framework (2006) is presented for each lesson.

### Activity introduction

Each lesson opens with a short introduction, designed to introduce the context of the lesson to the group (NB: these activities would not be suitable for the whole class). The introduction can also be used to review requirements in terms of mathematical understanding and to facilitate or scaffold thinking. Although the teacher will be at the centre of this section of the lesson, the main purpose is to pose questions and lines of enquiry for the children to develop during the main activity.

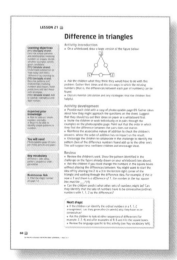

### Activity development

Incorporating instructions for setting and developing the main activity, this section offers opportunities for children to explain their thinking, so a range of teacher questions has been included. It is intended that the teacher will be at the perimeter of the group, allowing the children to maintain ownership of the learning, but will be available for low-level interventions. These include making observations, highlighting teaching/learning points, providing hints or tips for solving problems, suggesting methods of recording and so on.

### Review

This section is focused upon allowing children to explain their thinking or present their work, so that effective formative and summative assessment can be made. It also reviews all possible outcomes to an activity and summarises key learning points.

### Next steps

At the end of each lesson plan, ideas are included for how to develop an activity further. These ideas include at least one modification to an activity designed to challenge children and extend learning. This section also includes links to thinking skills and ICT.

## Characteristics of able children

An able child may demonstrate potential in a variety of ways:
● cognitive skills (for example, learning new ideas with extraordinary speed)
● speech and language, such as ability to follow a complex set of instructions
● learning styles (for example, logical approaches to problems)
● social, such as high expectations of self/others.

In mathematics, this might manifest itself through content (such as making links within and across different topics) and/or through process (for example, an aptitude for solving logical problems).

## Interventions

In extending able learners through challenge, pace and expectation, it is also important to consider the value of breadth of content. Most of the activities featured in this book include themes that all children in the class are likely to be exploring, albeit at a lower level of complexity. This feature enables the able child or group to integrate with the on-going topics of the class, and this serves an important social function.

An able child represents a challenge in terms of establishing the nature and extent of support. Broadly speaking, an able child needs every bit as much focus on learning as any other child. Through intervention and discussion, an able child can begin to appreciate what outcomes are expected or valued.

## Curriculum initiatives

One of the key objectives within *Excellence and Enjoyment* (DfES, 2004) was to support schools in taking ownership of the curriculum. This includes developing teaching programmes which support all groups, and in shaping the curriculum in ways which will maximise opportunity and achievement. Within this, the Primary National Strategy is seen as a vehicle to develop assessment for learning, providing knowledge about individual children to inform the way they are taught and learn. This book supports these aspirations by providing a measured approach to extending the more able child and, as appropriate, to engage directly with that individual in this process.

| Title of lesson | Year 1 objectives | Year 2 objectives | Tracking forward Year 3 objectives |
|---|---|---|---|
| 1. Cover half | Use/apply strand: Solve problems involving counting, adding, subtracting, doubling or halving. Counting strand: Use the vocabulary of halves and quarters. | Counting strand: Find one half, one quarter and three quarters of shapes and sets of objects. | |
| 2. Jump to 24 | Use/apply strand: Describe simple patterns and relationships involving numbers or shapes; decide whether examples satisfy given conditions. Knowledge strand: Count on or back in ones, twos, fives and tens. | Calculate strand: Represent repeated addition and arrays as multiplication, and sharing and repeated subtraction (grouping) as division; use practical and informal written methods to support multiplication and division, including calculations with remainders. | |
| 3. Three-digit number | Use/apply strand: Solve problems involving counting, adding, subtracting, doubling or halving. | Counting strand: Read and write two-digit and three-digit numbers in figures and words. | |
| 4. The broken necklace | Use/apply strand: Describe ways of solving puzzles and problems, explaining choices and decisions orally or using pictures. | Use/apply strand: Describe patterns and relationships involving numbers or shapes. Use/apply strand: Present solutions to puzzles and problems in an organised way. | |
| 5. Number grids | Use/apply strand: Describe simple patterns and relationships involving numbers or shapes. | Use/apply strand: Describe patterns and relationships involving numbers or shapes. Counting strand: Read and write two-digit and three-digit numbers in figures and words; describe and extend number sequences and recognise odd and even numbers. | |
| 6. Which pizza is whose? | Use/apply strand: Describe ways of solving puzzles and problems, explaining choices and decisions orally or using pictures. | Use/apply strand: Follow a line of enquiry; answer questions by choosing and using suitable equipment and selecting, organising and presenting information in lists, tables and simple diagrams. Counting strand: Find one half, one quarter and three quarters of shapes and sets of objects. | Use/apply strand: Follow a line of enquiry by deciding what information is important; make and use lists, tables and graphs to organise and interpret the information. |
| 7. Between and difference between | Use/apply strand: Solve problems involving counting, adding [and] subtracting. Counting strand: Compare and order numbers, using the related vocabulary. | Use/apply strand: Solve problems involving addition [and] subtraction. Counting strand: Order two-digit numbers and position them on a number line. | |
| 8. Petra's pet shop | Use/apply strand: Describe ways of solving puzzles and problems, explaining choices and decisions orally or using pictures. | Use/apply strand: Follow a line of enquiry; answer questions by choosing and using suitable equipment and selecting, organising and presenting information in lists, tables and simple diagrams. | |
| 9. Find the missing domino | Use/apply strand: Describe ways of solving puzzles and problems, explaining choices and decisions orally or using pictures. Counting strand: Compare and order numbers. | Use/apply strand: Describe patterns and relationships involving numbers or shapes. | |
| 10. Making money | Use/apply strand: Solve problems involving counting, adding, subtracting, doubling or halving in the context of numbers, measures or money. | Use/apply strand: Solve problems involving addition, subtraction, multiplication or division in contexts of numbers, measures or pounds and pence. | Counting strand: Partition three-digit numbers into multiples of 100, 10 and 1 in different ways. (Y4) Counting strand: Use decimal notation for tenths and hundredths and partition decimals. |
| 11. Busy bees | Use/apply strand: Solve problems involving counting. Counting strand: Compare and order numbers, using the related vocabulary. | Use/apply strand: Describe patterns and relationships involving numbers or shapes; make predictions and test these with examples. Counting strand: Order two-digit numbers and position them on a number line. | |
| 12. Marbles in pockets | Use/apply strand: Solve problems involving counting, adding, subtracting, doubling or halving in the context of numbers. | Use/apply strand: Present solutions to puzzles and problems in an organised way. Knowledge strand: Derive and recall all addition and subtraction facts for each number to at least 10, all pairs with totals to 20. | |
| 13. Multi-pairs | | Use/apply strand: Solve problems involving addition, subtraction, multiplication or division. | Knowledge strand: Derive and recall multiplication facts for the 2, 3, 4, 5, 6 and 10 times-tables and the corresponding division facts. |

| Title of lesson | Year 1 objectives | Year 2 objectives | Tracking forward Year 3 objectives |
|---|---|---|---|
| 14. More or less than 500? | | **Knowledge strand:** Derive and recall all addition and subtraction facts for each number to at least 10, all pairs with totals to 20 and all pairs of multiples of 10 with totals up to 100. | **Counting strand:** Round two-digit or three-digit numbers to the nearest 10 or 100 and give estimates for their sums and differences. |
| 15. Fraction necklace | | **Use/apply strand:** Describe patterns and relationships involving numbers or shapes, make predictions and test these with examples.<br>**Counting strand:** Find one half, one quarter and three quarters of shapes and sets of objects. | **Use/apply strand:** Describe and explain methods, choices and solutions to puzzles and problems, orally and in writing, using pictures and diagrams. |
| 16. Name patterns | | **Use/apply strand:** Describe patterns and relationships involving numbers or shapes, make predictions and test these with examples.<br>**Counting strand:** Read and write two-digit and three-digit numbers in figures and words; describe and extend number sequences and recognise odd and even numbers.<br>**Knowledge strand:** Derive and recall multiplication facts for the 2, 5 and 10 times-tables and the related division facts; recognise multiples of 2, 5 and 10. | **Use/apply strand:** Identify patterns and relationships involving numbers or shapes, and use these to solve problems. |
| 17. Ten hens in pens | **Knowledge strand:** Count on or back in tens and use this knowledge to derive the multiples of 10 to the tenth multiple. | **Knowledge strand:** Derive and recall all pairs of multiples of 10 with totals up to 100.<br>**Knowledge strand:** Recognise multiples of 2, 5 and 10. | **Knowledge strand:** Derive and recall sums and differences of multiples of 10 and number pairs that total 100. |
| 18. Double trouble | **Knowledge strand:** Count on or back in ones, twos, fives and tens and use this knowledge to derive the multiples of 2, 5 and 10 to the tenth multiple.<br>**Knowledge strand:** Recall the doubles of numbers to at least 10. | **Knowledge strand:** Understand that halving is the inverse of doubling and derive and recall doubles of all numbers to 20, and the corresponding halves. | **Knowledge strand:** Derive and recall all addition and subtraction facts for each number to 20, sums and differences of multiples of 10 and number pairs that total 100. |
| 19. Postman Jim | | **Use/apply strand:** Solve problems involving addition [and] subtraction.<br>**Calculate strand:** Add or subtract mentally a one-digit number... to or from any two-digit number. | |
| 20. The toy shop | | **Use/apply strand:** Identify and record the information or calculation needed to solve a puzzle or problem; carry out the steps or calculations and check the solution.<br>**Calculate strand:** Use the symbols +, −, ×, ÷ and = to record and interpret number sentences involving all four operations. | |
| 21. Difference in triangles | **Use/apply strand:** Describe simple patterns and relationships involving numbers or shapes; decide whether examples satisfy given conditions.<br>**Calculate strand:** Understand subtraction as 'take away' and find a 'difference' by counting up. | **Use/apply strand:** Describe patterns and relationships involving numbers and shapes, make predictions and test these with examples.<br>**Calculate strand:** Add or subtract mentally a one-digit number. | |
| 22. Build a model | | **Use/apply strand:** Solve problems involving addition, subtraction, multiplication or division in contexts of numbers, measures or pounds and pence.<br>**Calculate strand:** Add or subtract mentally a one-digit number or a multiple of 10 to or from any two-digit number; use practical and informal written methods to add and subtract two-digit numbers. | |
| 23. Fraction pairs | | **Use/apply strand:** Solve problems involving addition, subtraction, multiplication or division in contexts of numbers. | **Calculate strand:** Find unit fractions of numbers and quantities (for example, $\frac{1}{2}$, $\frac{1}{4}$ and $\frac{1}{6}$ of 12 litres). |
| 24. Arrays | | **Use/apply strand:** Solve problems involving addition, subtraction, multiplication or division in contexts of numbers.<br>**Calculate strand:** Represent repeated addition and arrays as multiplication. | |
| 25. Make a sentence | **Use/apply strand:** Answer a question by selecting and sorting information. | **Use/apply strand:** Identify and record the information or calculation needed to solve a puzzle or problem; carry out the steps or calculations and check the solution.<br>**Calculate strand:** Use the symbols +, −, ×, ÷ and = to record and interpret number sentences involving all four operations; calculate the value of an unknown in a number sentence. | **Calculate strand:** Add or subtract mentally combinations of one-digit and two-digit numbers. |

| Title of lesson | Year 1 objectives | Year 2 objectives | Tracking forward Year 3 objectives |
|---|---|---|---|
| **26. More or less** | **Counting strand:** Say the number that is 1 more or 1 less than any given number, and 10 more or less for multiples of 10. | **Calculate strand:** Add or subtract mentally a one-digit number or a multiple of 10 to or from any two-digit number; use practical and informal written methods to add and subtract two-digit numbers. | **Use/apply strand:** Follow a line of enquiry by deciding what information is important; make and use lists, tables and graphs to organise and interpret the information. |
| **27. Subtraction sacks** | **Calculate strand:** Understand subtraction as 'take away' and find a 'difference' by counting up.<br>**Calculate strand:** Use the vocabulary related to addition and subtraction and symbols to describe and record addition and subtraction number sentences. | **Calculate strand:** Understand that subtraction is the inverse of addition and vice versa; use this to derive and record related addition and subtraction number sentences.<br>**Use/apply strand:** Present solutions to puzzles and problems in an organised way. | |
| **28. Investigating triangles** | | **Use/apply strand:** Describe patterns and relationships involving numbers or shapes, make predictions and test these with examples.<br>**Shape strand:** Visualise common 2D shapes; sort, make and describe shapes, referring to their properties. | |
| **29. Walk to school** | **Use/apply strand:** Describe a puzzle or problem using numbers, practical materials and diagrams; use these to solve the problem and set the solution in the original context. | **Shape strand:** Follow and give instructions involving position, direction and movement. | |
| **30. Making shapes from squares** | | **Use/apply strand:** Describe patterns and relationships involving numbers or shapes, make predictions and test these with examples.<br>**Shape strand:** Follow and give instructions involving position, direction and movement. | **Use/apply strand:** Follow a line of enquiry by deciding what information is important; make and use lists, tables and graphs to organise and interpret the information.<br>**Use/apply strand:** Describe and explain methods, choices and solutions to puzzles and problems, orally and in writing, using pictures and diagrams. |
| **31. Trying triangles** | **Use/apply strand:** Describe simple patterns and relationships involving numbers or shapes. | **Use/apply strand:** Describe patterns and relationships involving numbers or shapes, make predictions and test these with examples.<br>**Shape strand:** Visualise common 2D shapes; identify shapes from pictures of them in different positions and orientations; sort, make and describe shapes, referring to their properties. | **Use/apply strand:** Identify patterns and relationships involving numbers or shapes, and use these to solve problems. |
| **32. Square crazy** | **Measure strand:** Estimate, measure, weigh and compare objects, choosing and using suitable uniform non-standard or standard units and measuring instruments. | **Use/apply strand:** Describe patterns and relationships involving numbers or shapes, make predictions and test these with examples.<br>**Measure strand:** Estimate, compare and measure lengths, weights and capacities, choosing and using standard units. | **(Y4) Measure strand:** Draw rectangles and measure and calculate their perimeters; find the area of rectilinear shapes drawn on a square grid by counting squares. |
| **33. Dinner ladies** | **Use/apply strand:** Describe simple patterns and relationships involving numbers or shapes; decide whether examples satisfy given conditions. | **Use/apply strand:** Describe patterns and relationships involving numbers or shapes, make predictions and test these with examples. | **Shape strand:** Read and record the vocabulary of position, direction and movement. |
| **34. Counterton map** | | **Shape strand:** Follow and give instructions involving position, direction and movement. | **Use/apply strand:** Follow a line of enquiry by deciding what information is important.<br>**Shape strand:** Read and record the vocabulary of position, direction and movement, using the four compass directions to describe movement about a grid. |
| **35. Cube puzzle** | **Shape strand:** Identify objects that turn about a point or about a line; recognise and make whole, half and quarter turns. | **Shape strand:** Identify reflective symmetry in patterns and 2D shapes and draw lines of symmetry in shapes. | **Shape strand:** Draw and complete shapes with reflective symmetry; draw the reflection of a shape in a mirror line along one side. |
| **36. Shape double** | | **Use/apply strand:** Follow a line of enquiry; answer questions by choosing and using suitable equipment and selecting, organising and presenting information.<br>**Measure strand:** Estimate, compare and measure lengths... using standard units. | |

| Title of lesson | Year 1 objectives | Year 2 objectives | Tracking forward Year 3 objectives |
|---|---|---|---|
| 37. Go fishing | | **Use/apply strand:** Solve problems involving addition, subtraction, multiplication or division in contexts of numbers. **Measure strand:** Estimate, compare and measure lengths... using standard units and suitable measuring instruments. | |
| 38. Ribbons | **Use/apply strand:** Answer a question by selecting and using suitable equipment, and sorting information, shapes or objects. | **Measure strand:** Estimate, compare and measure lengths... using standard units. | |
| 39. The hungry bug | | **Use/apply strand:** Solve problems involving addition. **Measure strand:** Estimate, compare and measure lengths, weights and capacities, choosing and using standard units. | |
| 40. Tetrominoes | | **Use/apply strand:** Describe patterns and relationships involving numbers or shapes, make predictions and test these with examples. **Shape strand:** Visualise common 2D shapes and 3D solids; identify shapes from pictures of them in different positions and orientations; sort, make and describe shapes. | |
| 41. Bedtime | | **Use/apply strand:** Solve problems involving addition, subtraction, multiplication or division. **Measure strand:** Use units of time and know the relationships between them; read the time to the quarter hour; identify time intervals. | |
| 42. Equi-match dominoes | **Measure strand:** Estimate, measure, weigh and compare objects, choosing and using suitable standard units and measuring instruments. | **Measure strand:** Estimate, compare and measure lengths, weights and capacities, choosing and using standard units. | **Measure strand:** Know the relationships between kilometres and metres, metres and centimetres, kilograms and grams, litres and millilitres. |
| 43. Dates, days and months | **Measure strand:** Use vocabulary related to time; order days of the week and months. | **Measure strand:** Use units of time and know the relationships between them. | **Measure strand:** Calculate time intervals and find start or end times for a given time interval. |
| 44. Vegetable plot | | **Use/apply strand:** Solve problems involving addition, subtraction, multiplication or division in contexts of numbers [and] measures. **Measure strand:** Estimate, compare and measure lengths, choosing and using standard units. | **Measure strand:** Know the relationships between... metres and centimetres. |
| 45. Flower garden | **Use/apply strand:** Solve problems involving counting, adding, subtracting, doubling or halving in the context of numbers. **Data strand:** Use diagrams to sort objects into groups according to a given criterion. | | |
| 46. Domino sort | | **Use/apply strand:** Follow a line of enquiry; answer questions by choosing and using suitable equipment and selecting, organising and presenting information. **Data strand:** Use lists, tables and diagrams to sort objects; explain choices using appropriate language, including 'not'. | |
| 47. Train timetable | | **Use/apply strand:** Follow a line of enquiry; answer questions by choosing and using suitable equipment and selecting, organising and presenting information. **Data strand:** Answer a question by collecting and recording data in lists and tables. | |
| 48. Number sort | | **Use/apply strand:** Follow a line of enquiry; answer questions by choosing and using suitable equipment and selecting, organising and presenting information. **Data strand:** Use lists, tables and diagrams to sort objects; explain choices using appropriate language, including 'not'. | |
| 49. Wizard hats | **Use/apply strand:** Solve problems involving counting. **Use/apply strand:** Describe ways of solving puzzles and problems, explaining choices and decisions. | **Use/apply strand:** Identify and record the information or calculation needed to solve a puzzle or problem; carry out the steps or calculations and check the solution. **Use/apply strand:** Present solutions to problems in an organised way; explain decisions, methods and results. | |
| 50. Packed lunch recycle | **Data strand:** Answer a question by recording information in lists and tables; present outcomes using practical resources. | **Data strand:** Use lists, tables and diagrams to sort objects; explain choices using appropriate language, including 'not'. | **Data strand:** Answer a question by collecting, organising and interpreting data; use... pictograms and bar charts to represent results. |

## SELF-ASSESSMENT 🗌 RECORDING SHEET

Name: _____  Date: _____

| Activity title: | | | |
|---|---|---|---|
| **I can** _____ _____ _____ _____ _____ _____ _____ | 👍 | ✊ | 👎 |
| **I was able to** _____ _____ _____ _____ _____ _____ | 👍 | ✊ | 👎 |

| I can |
|---|
| _____ |
| _____ |
| _____ |

50 MATHS LESSONS FOR MORE ABLE LEARNERS · AGES 5-7

**PHOTOCOPIABLE** ■**SCHOLASTIC**
www.scholastic.co.uk

| | Use/apply strand | Counting strand | Knowledge strand | Calculate strand | Shape strand | Measure strand | Data strand |
|---|---|---|---|---|---|---|---|
| 1. In the bag | ● | | ● | | | | |
| 2. The last penny | ● | | | ● | | | |
| 3. Make 12 | ● | | ● | | | | |
| 4. Find the magic number | ● | | | ● | | | |
| 5. Add 10 or double | ● | | | ● | | | |
| 6. Crack the code | ● | | | | ● | | |
| 7. What's my rule? | ● | | | ● | | | |
| 8. Is it true? (1) | ● | | | | | | |
| 9. Is it true? (2) | ● | ● | | | ● | | |
| 10. The answer is... | ● | | | ● | | | |
| 11. How many words? | ● | ● | | | | | ● |
| 12. Number bond suits | ● | | ● | | | | |
| 13. Shoe size | ● | | | | | ● | |
| 14. Football kit | ● | ● | | ● | | | |
| 15. Clothes size | ● | | | | | ● | |
| 16. Birthday money | ● | ● | | ● | | | |
| 17. How many? | ● | ● | | | | | ● |
| 18. How many numbers? | ● | ● | | | | | |
| 19. Rough snack symmetry | ● | | | | ● | | |
| 20. I spy a shape | ● | | | | ● | | |

# Brainteasers

## 1 In the bag

**Learning objective**
(Y2) Knowledge strand: Derive and recall all addition and subtraction facts for each number to at least 10.

**Thinking skill:** Reasoning about number.

**What to do:** The game presented on page 18 requires the players to recognise and use their knowledge of number bonds to 10 and identify an unknown. Ensure that each player has a turn in predicting how many bricks are in the bag.

**Outcomes:** The game provides practice in the recall of number bonds to 10. This is an important skill and can be applied to calculation with larger numbers. If number bonds are unknown, then alternative strategies can be used, such as counting up from the known number to 10, while keeping track of the count. The activity also provides an opportunity for the identification of an unknown, and developing strategies to solve problems in the form of $6 + \square = 10$.

**Probing questions:** If there are six bricks on the table, how many are in the bag? How do you know that there are four bricks in the bag?

**Next step:** Play the game with a smaller or larger number of bricks.

## 2 The last penny

**Learning objective**
(Y2) Use/apply strand: Solve problems involving addition, subtraction, multiplication or division.

**Thinking skill:** Reasoning about number.

**What to do:** Read through the challenge with the group or child and ensure that they understand the objective of the task.

**Outcomes:** This game requires players to develop a strategy to win. The game should be played several times to allow this to happen. The strategy is to recognise that the player who leaves three coins towards the end of the game will on their next turn be in a position to take the last penny as the other player is forced to leave one or two coins.

**Probing question:** If it is your turn and there are four coins remaining, how many will you take?

**Next step:** Change the number of coins. Change the number allowed to be taken away to 3 or 4.

**Learning objective**
**(Y2) Knowledge strand:** Derive and recall all addition and subtraction facts for each number to at least 10.

# 3 Make 12

**Thinking skills:** Trying out ideas and recognising the relationship between numbers.

**What to do:** The activity outlined on page 19 requires children to use a trial and improvement method until each row and column totals 12. It is essential that children are able to move the numbers around, so they need to be cut out or number cards used in their place.

**Outcomes:** The solution to the problem requires the numbers to be in the following order, moving across, down and then across the grid: 7,2,3,4,5,6,1. The order may also be reversed.

**Probing question:** How many ways can you make 12, using three numbers between 1 and 7?

**Next step:** If necessary, you could simplify the activity by inserting the 4 and/or the 5 into the grid.

**Learning objective**
**(Y2) Use/apply strand:** Solve problems involving addition, subtraction, multiplication or division.

# 4 Find the magic number

**Thinking skills:** Trying out ideas and reasoning about number.

**What to do:** This activity is similar to the previous one and requires the same strategy. This time, however, the magic number is unknown.

**Outcomes:** The magic number is 9, the total of each row and column. The middle number is 3 and the pairs of numbers either side are 2 and 4 and 1 and 5.

**Probing questions:** Which numbers go together? Would it make sense to put both the 4 and 5 in the row? (No, because these are the two largest numbers and so would make the total of the row larger than the total of the column.)

**Next step:** Extend the arms of the cross by adding a square to each end. Ask the children to place the numbers 6, 7, 8 and 9 in these squares so that the row and column add up to the same total.

**Learning objective**
**(Y1) Calculate strand:** Use practical and informal written methods to support the addition of a one-digit number or a multiple of 10 to a one-digit or two-digit number.

# 5 Add 10 or double

**Thinking skill:** Decision-making based on reasoning.

**What to do:** The numbers ranging from 1-9 need to be randomly selected. This could be by using a 1-9 dice or 1-9 digit cards in a bag. The children should make a reasoned decision as to whether it is best to add 10 or double the number. Resources such as a number line or square may be required to support calculation. Encourage the children to use their understanding of place value to add 10.

**Outcomes:** The winner is the first person to cover four numbers in a row.

**Probing question:** Is it possible to cover an odd number on the grid by using a doubling strategy?

**Next step:** The game could continue until all numbers are covered, the winner being the person with the most spaces covered.

# 6 Crack the code

**Thinking skill:** Identifying relationships between numbers.

**What to do:** Each row, column and diagonal adds up to the same total. The children need to identify the value of the circle, square and triangle.

**Outcomes:** There is more than one solution to this problem but all the solutions are related. The simplest solution is: circle = 1, triangle = 2 and square = 3 and the total is 6. Any three numbers with the same ratio (for example, 2, 4 and 6 resulting in a total of 12) will also work.

If the children find just one solution, challenge them to find another. This should support them in seeing the relationship between solutions and prepare them for future work on ratio.

**Probing questions:** If the answer is 1, 2 and 3, will 3, 6 and 9 work? What is the relationship between the numbers?

**Next step:** The activity can be extended by asking the children to find alternative solutions to the problem.

**Learning objective**
(Y2) Use/apply strand: Describe patterns and relationships involving numbers or shapes.

# 7 What's my rule?

**Thinking skill:** Identifying relationships between numbers.

**What to do:** The activity presented on photocopiable page 21 uses the idea of two function machines. A number is put into the first machine, an operation performed and the result comes out. This number then goes into the second machine, another operation is performed and the number comes out. If the children have not met a function machine previously, you may want to give them an activity that uses just one machine with one operation before they tackle the two-step problem.

**Outcomes:** Children will find a variety of solutions such as add 1, and then add 2 or double and add 1.

**Probing question:** What would happen if you put 100 into the machines?

**Next step:** In pairs, encourage the children to devise their own function machines, deciding which operation should be used in each machine. They can swap their machines with another pair and work out the rules.

**Learning objective**
(Y2) Use/apply strand: Solve problems involving addition, subtraction, multiplication or division.

# 8 Is it true? (1)

**Thinking skill:** Investigating the properties of number.

**What to do:** For the first statement, encourage the children to provide examples and to generalise whether the question is true or untrue. For example, it is true when both numbers are more than 5. For the second statement, again encourage the children to provide examples and generalise. A multiple of 2 will always be even as it represents the addition of even numbers. Practical materials such as cubes may enable a child to demonstrate this and provide a convincing argument that it will always be true. A multiple of 3, however, is not always odd. Again, encourage examples and recognition that the 3 times-table produces an odd, even, odd, even pattern.

**Outcomes:** These two questions are intended to stimulate thinking and lead to investigation.

**Probing questions:** Is 200 an odd or even number? How do you know?

**Next step:** Investigate odd and even patterns in other multiples.

**Learning objective**
(Y2) Use/apply strand: Follow a line of enquiry; answer questions by choosing and using suitable equipment and selecting, organising and presenting information in lists, tables and simple diagrams.

**Learning objective**
(Y1) **Shape strand:** Visualise and name common 2D shapes and describe their features.

# 9 Is it true? (2)

**Thinking skill:** Reasoning about the properties of shape.

**What to do:** Read through the questions on page 22 with the group or child and ensure that they understand the objective of the task.

**Outcomes:** These two questions should encourage the children to consider in greater detail the properties of squares and rectangles and where these overlap. They should be able to reason that a square is in fact a rectangle as it has all the properties of a rectangle (four straight sides, four right angles and opposite sides are parallel). The second statement should enable the children to recognise that the term 'longer' is relative. Although they may initially think that a rectangle is longer as it is 'a long thin object', a square can be longer.

**Probing question:** If a square is longer than a rectangle, is it also wider?

**Next step:** Rectangles and squares are both quadrilaterals as they have four sides. Can the children identify any other quadrilaterals in the classroom?

**Learning objective**
(Y2) **Use/apply strand:** Solve problems involving addition, subtraction, multiplication or division.

# 10 The answer is...

**Thinking skill:** Decision-making.

**What to do:** Encourage the children to use both addition and subtraction to obtain an answer of 24. There are also some answers involving multiplication. Division is a little more difficult but may be attempted by some children (for example, $48 \div 2 = 24$).

**Outcomes:** This is an open investigation where there are an infinite number of answers.

**Probing question:** Can you find three numbers that total 24?

**Next step:** In pairs, invite the children to think up their own 'The answer is...' number mystery. They can swap their answers with another pair and challenge them to discover the question.

**Learning objective**
(Y1) **Use/apply strand:** Describe ways of solving puzzles and problems, explaining choices and decisions orally and in writing.

# 11 How many words?

**Thinking skills:** Logic and reasoning about number.

**What to do:** Present the children with a small selection of books. Build on the questions on page 23. Discuss what the children need to know, and how they are going to effectively estimate the number of words in a particular book (you will obviously need to select appropriate books). Encourage children who could be moved on to multiplying numbers rather than repeated addition as appropriate. Offer appropriate thinking and discussion time before gathering ideas.

**Outcomes:** The children will develop a range of problem-solving skills through collaborative working and thinking. They will also be able to extend logical ideas and processes to estimate large numbers.

**Probing questions:** How many words are in a book? How will you count the words in a book? How can you avoid mistakes in counting?

**Next step:** You can adapt the activity as appropriate to the ability of the children. Familiar books can be particularly motivating for the children – for example, what the class is reading in literacy lessons or what you are reading to them in story time, and favourite story books.

## Learning objectives
**(Y1) Knowledge strand:** Derive and recall all pairs of numbers with a total of 10.
**(Y2) Knowledge strand:** Derive and recall all pairs with totals to 20.

# 12 Number bond suits

**Thinking skill:** Recalling facts quickly.

**What to do:** Read through the instructions on page 23 with the group or child and ensure that they understand the objective of the task (the game can also be played with two players instead of three, and using 1–20 number cards instead of the playing cards).

**Outcomes:** Children will feel secure in their knowledge and confidence in remembering and recalling number bonds of 10 and 20.

**Probing questions:** What do we need to know by heart? What do we do if we are not sure of an answer? If we do not know the answer, how can we work it out?

**Next step:** Challenge the children to work out their number bonds of 11, 12, 13 and so on.

## Learning objectives
**(Y1) Measure strand:** Estimate, measure and compare objects using suitable uniform units.
**(Y2) Measure strand:** Estimate, compare and measure lengths using standard units.

# 13 Shoe size

**Thinking skills:** Reasoning and logical processes.

**What to do:** Use three differently styled shoes borrowed from the children (or lost property) and talk about their style of design, fabric/materials and construction. Ask the questions on page 24 and discuss with the children their thoughts on how shoes are made in different sizes. Encourage them to predict then measure the shoes together.

**Outcomes:** Children will begin to understand some of the differences and similarities in people. They will also start to think about the different materials and use for purpose (cross-curricular).

**Probing questions:** Are all shoes the same length? Are they all the same width? Does it matter what they are made of?

**Next step:** Take three different-sized shoes and estimate what the difference in measurements might be. They could be measured by drawing around the sole of the shoes and then measuring and calculating the differences between each sized shoe.

## Learning objectives
**(Y2) Use/apply strand:** Solve problems involving addition and multiplication in context.
**(Y2) Use/apply strand:** Follow a line of enquiry (and present findings).

# 14 Football kit

**Thinking skills:** Problem-solving using logical thinking and collaboration.

**What to do:** Explain to the children that if the school has a football team, they usually all wear the same clothes. Discuss the differences of any sport they know about. Ask what a football team needs to wear to play. Get them to think about moving to multiplying and/or doubling numbers from simple counting. There is an opportunity to introduce division through looking at pairs of socks and individual socks. Is there a left and right sock? (Not in sports socks unless they have a logo on one side - having an example would be helpful here.)

**Outcomes:** Children will be able to count in multiples, beginning to use doubles for a purpose (for example, two socks for one person).

**Probing questions:** How many people make a team? Is it the same in all sports? How many people are in a football team? What kit do footballers wear? How many shirts do you need for a team? What if you had two teams or three, how many shirts and shorts would you need?

**Next step:** Look at other sports teams and the number of players/amount of kit needed.

**Learning objective**
(Y2) **Measure strand:** Estimate, compare and measure lengths, choosing and using standard units and suitable measuring instruments.

# 15 Clothes size

**Thinking skills:** Problem-solving using reasoning and logical thinking.

**What to do:** Show the children the two illustrations on page 25. Ask them what size the Little Bear's clothes in the picture might be. Discuss how they can find out. Measure one of the pictures using appropriate vocabulary (length and width) and then estimate the measurements of the other picture. Ask the children to measure it. Use real items of clothing of a similar size to the children in your class (for example, three PE shirts of different sizes from lost property or borrowed from the children). Display the items and ask the children what sizes they are. Discuss the size on the labels in relation to national sizes, then ask small groups or pairs to estimate the length and width (in centimetres) of one or all of the shirts. Measure the shirts when the time is up to compare children's estimates.

**Outcomes:** Children will begin to know the difference between length and width, measuring accurately in centimetres. They will also develop an understanding of sizes of clothing.

**Probing questions:** What size do you think these shirts are? What do you estimate the length of this shirt is? What about the width?

**Next step:** Use a different item of clothing for the activity, such as winter coats. They will vary in length and padded coats will give the illusion of being bigger, as well as offering the discussion of whether to include hoods as part of the coat's length.

**Learning objective**
(Y2): **Calculate strand:** Add mentally a one-digit number or a multiple of 10 to or from any two-digit number; use practical and informal written methods to add two-digit numbers.

# 16 Birthday money

**Thinking skill:** Investigating large numbers.

**What to do:** Explain to the children that they got £100 for their birthday from all their many uncles and aunts, friends and family. Ask them to look at page 25 and discuss the items they would like to buy with their money. Encourage them to think about: the price of each item; what they could buy; how many items they could buy; how much change they would have.

**Outcomes:** Children will become familiar with larger sums of money, thinking about real-life prices of toys ending in £0.99. They will also consider the value of £100.

**Probing questions:** How much does each item cost? What could you buy from the catalogue with £100? Is there any money left over? What change would you have? Could you buy something else?

**Next step:** Change the costing amounts of the items to suit your particular group of children, or use a shop catalogue instead of the pupil page. This way you can adapt the prices and questions to your own class's needs.

**Learning objectives**
(Y2) **Counting strand:** Estimate a number of objects; round two-digit numbers to the nearest 10.
(Y3) **Counting strand:** Round two-digit or three-digit numbers to the nearest 10 or 100 and give estimates for their sums and differences.

# 17 How many?

**Thinking skills:** Logical processes.

**What to do:** Provide some real cereal and bowls for this activity to emphasise the real-life element. Ask the children to estimate the number of items of (large-pieced) cereal that could be poured into the bowl. Pour the cereal and ask if their estimation has changed. Offer thinking and discussion time.

**Outcomes:** Children will begin to estimate large numbers using real-life objects. They will also begin to understand the value of estimation to answer questions about real life and time frames.

**Probing questions:** How many pieces of cereal do you estimate the bowl holds? How will you count them? How can you avoid mistakes in counting?

**Next step:** Pose extended problems: if you ate (x) amount of cereal every day, how many would you eat in a week? A month? A year?

# 18 How many numbers?

**Thinking skill:** Reasoning about number.

**What to do:** Explain that the aim of the activity is to make as many numbers as possible using the three digits supplied on page 26.

**Outcomes:** The three digits can make six three-digit numbers, six two-digit numbers and three single-digit numbers (a total of 15 different numbers).

**Probing questions:** How many different three-digit numbers can you make? How many two-digit numbers can you make? How many one-digit, two-digit and three-digit numbers can be made with these three digits?

**Next step:** Vary the choice of digits. Include a zero in your chosen digits to emphasise place holders.

## Learning objectives
**(Y2) Counting strand:** Explain what each digit in a two-digit number represents.
**(Y3) Counting strand:** Order whole numbers to at least a 1000.

# 19 Rough snack symmetry

**Thinking skills:** Visualising shapes and logical thinking.

**What to do:** Using snacks such as fruit, vegetables, biscuits and so on, discuss the different shapes with the children: whole shapes, half and cut shapes. Ask the children to visualise the shapes before you cut them. Do the snacks have lines of symmetry?

**Outcomes:** Children will begin to think about how shapes change when sliced and visualise what the shape would look like if sliced a different way.

**Probing questions:** What shape is this? Does it have any symmetry? What shape will appear when I cut it?

**Next step:** Draw the shape on the board and add the line(s) of symmetry. If appropriate, discuss the accuracy of drawings and items. For example, is an apple a perfect sphere?

## Learning objectives
**(Y2) Shape strand:** Visualise common 2D shapes and 3D solids; identify them in different orientations.
**(Y2) Shape strand:** Identify reflective symmetry in patterns and 2D shapes.

# 20 I spy a shape

**Thinking skills:** Reasoning and logical processes.

**What to do:** This activity is an excellent tool to develop effective questioning skills related to 3D shapes. Show the illustration on page 27 (or even better, use real items in front of the children). Now play a game of 'I Spy'. Say: *I spy with my little eye, something that has a triangle face.* Encourage the children to ask questions (using mathematical vocabulary) to eliminate or detect the shape you are thinking of.

**Outcomes:** Children will become familiar with the shapes in everyday objects and relate them to mathematical shapes and correct vocabulary.

**Probing questions:** What are useful questions to ask in a game of 'I Spy'? What sort of questions could be asked?

**Next step:** Limit the number of questions that can be asked before the shape is identified. When the children become familiar with the game, ask one of them to choose an item for the rest of the class/group to identify through questioning.

## Learning objective
**(Y2) Shape strand:** Describe shapes, referring to their properties.

# 1: In the bag

■ Ask your friend to count the bricks and then close their eyes. Put some of the bricks in the bag. By just looking at the bricks left on the table, can your friend tell you how many bricks are in the bag?

# 2: The last penny

■ Play with a friend. In turn, take either one or two pennies. The aim is to be the person to take the last penny.

**PHOTOCOPIABLE** ■SCHOLASTIC
www.scholastic.co.uk

# 3: Make 12

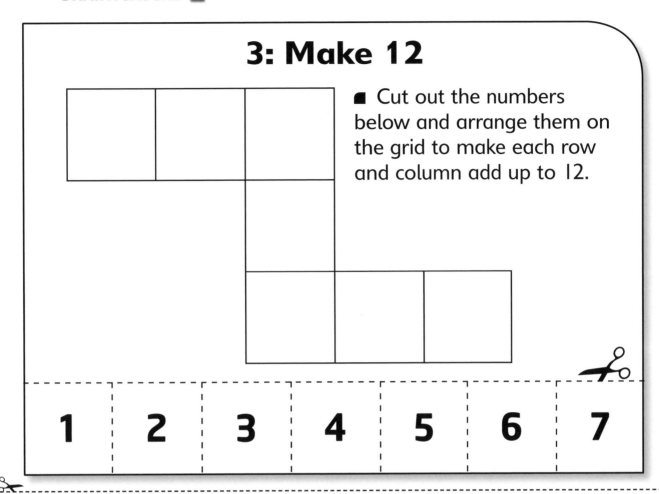

■ Cut out the numbers below and arrange them on the grid to make each row and column add up to 12.

1  2  3  4  5  6  7

# 4: Find the magic number

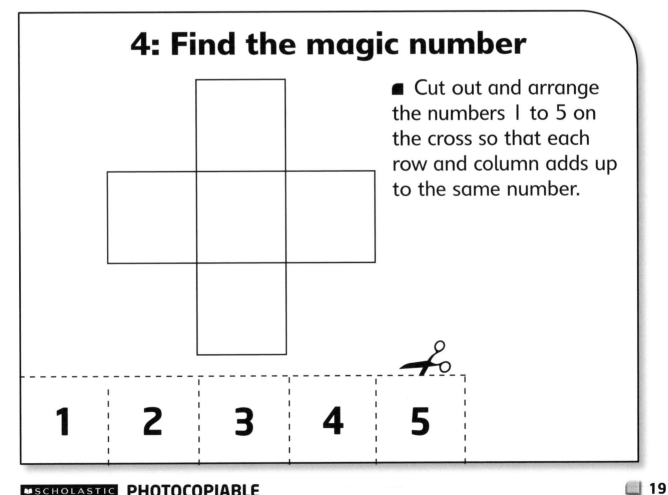

■ Cut out and arrange the numbers 1 to 5 on the cross so that each row and column adds up to the same number.

1  2  3  4  5

# 5: Add 10 or double

| 16 | 11 | 14 | 17 |
|----|----|----|----|
| 10 | 18 | 16 | 15 |
| 8  | 14 | 12 | 13 |
| 12 | 16 | 19 | 6  |

■ Roll a 1–9 dice. Add 10 to this number or double it. Cover the result on the grid. The winner is the first person to get 4 in a row.

# 6: Crack the code

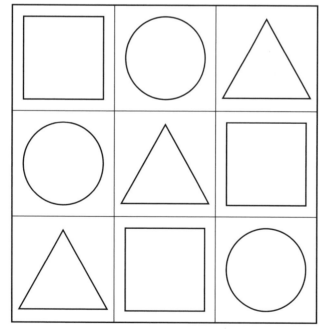

■ Each row, column and diagonal adds up to the same total.
■ What is the value of:

■ Is there more than one answer?

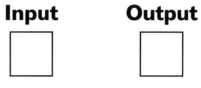

# 7: What's my rule?

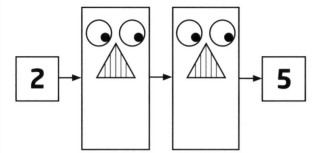

**Input**  **Output**

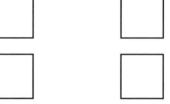

◾ A number goes through two function machines. Each machine has a rule that changes the number. Can you work out what they are? Add some more inputs and outputs.

# 8: Is it true? (1)

◾ Two numbers less than 10 always make a number more than 10.

◾ A multiple of 2 is always even. A multiple of 3 is always odd.

Illustration © Gaynor Berry

# 9: Is it true? (2)

◀ A square is a rectangle.

◀ A rectangle is longer than a square.

Illustration © Gaynor Berry

---

# 10: The answer is...

◀ What is the question?

Illustration © Gaynor Berry

# 11: How many words?

◾ How many words are in a book?

◾ Choose a book from the reading corner.

◾ What sort of information do you need to know before trying to answer this question?

◾ Does it matter if it is a fiction or non-fiction book? What is the difference between them?

◾ What will help you to estimate the number of words?

Illustration © Gaynor Berry

✂ - - - - - - - - - - - - - - - - - - - - - - - - - - - - - - - - - - - - - - - - - - - - - - - - - - - - - - - -

# 12: Number bond suits

◾ Game for three or more players.

◾ Using playing cards, sort out cards 1–10 (using the Ace as 1) in a pack and shuffle them.

◾ One player is the Bond Checker; the others play the game until all the cards are won. Take turns in being the Bond Checker.

◾ The Bond Checker turns over the first card. The first person to call out its bond to 10 (for example, if a 3 is laid down, a player must call out '7', as 3 + 7 = 10). The Bond Checker checks the call and awards the card to the first person to call the correct answer.

◾ The winner is the player with the most cards.

◾ Now include Jack as 11, Queen as 12 and King as 13. Play the game again and find number bonds to 20.

Illustration © Gaynor Berry

# 13: Shoe size

◾ Do all size 10 shoes measure the same?
◾ Look at the outside of the shoes. Do they look the same length? Width? Do they have the same-sized sole if you draw around them on paper?

*Illustration © Gaynor Berry*

# 14: Football kit

◾ What is a kit?

◾ How many items do you have to buy to kit out the school team?
◾ Do you need any spare kit?

*Illustration © Gaynor Berry*

# 15: Clothes size

**Little Bear**          **Big Bear**

# 16: Birthday money

| | | | |
|---|---|---|---|
| £48.99 | £14.99 | £85.49 | £41.99 |
| £11.99 | £24.99 | £34.99 | £89.99 |

Illustration © Gaynor Berry

# 17: How many?

■ How many pieces of cereal can you get in your breakfast bowl?

*Illustration © Gaynor Berry*

# 18: How many numbers?

| 2 | 6 | 9 |
|---|---|---|

■ How many numbers can I make with these three digits?

*Illustration © Gaynor Berry*

# 19: Rough snack symmetry

- Which snacks have symmetry?
- Which have no symmetry?
- Where are the (rough) lines of symmetry?

# 20: I spy a shape

# Cover half

**Learning objectives**
(Y1) Use/apply strand:
Solve problems involving
counting, adding,
subtracting, doubling or
halving in the context of
numbers.
(Y1) Counting strand: Use
the vocabulary of halves
and quarters in context.
(Y2) Counting strand: Find
one half, one quarter and
three quarters of shapes
and sets of objects.

**Expected prior
knowledge**
● Understand the concept
of a half in the context of
both number and shape.

**You will need**
Photocopiable page 29 (one
per child); 2cm cubes (20
per child).

**Key vocabulary**
half, odd, even

**Brainteaser link**
8: 'Is it true? (1)' on page
13.

## Activity introduction
● Ask each child to cover half of the snake on photocopiable page 29 with cubes.
● Ask: *How many cubes did it take to cover half of the snake? How many squares remain uncovered?* Establish that the answer is six.
● Ask: *Is there more than one way to cover half the snake?* Establish that it does not matter which squares are covered as long as there are six and that, to represent a half, the same number needs to be covered as uncovered.

## Activity development
● Ask the children to complete the activity on the photocopiable sheet.
● Ask questions: *Is it possible to cover half of a snake made from 13 squares? Which snakes can be half covered? Can a snake with six squares or seven squares* [and so on] *be half covered?*
● Establish that only snakes with an even number of squares can be half covered by cubes.
● Children could make a list of those snakes that could be half covered and those that could not. Encourage consideration of larger numbers up to 100 and possibly beyond.

## Review
● Bring together information collected by the children relating to which snakes can be half covered and make a list.
● The activity should have resulted in a list of odd and even numbers. Children should have made the connection that only even numbers can be halved. Indeed, this is the definition of an even number: a number that can be divided into two equal parts.
● As children progress in the activity they may no longer need the support of cubes to identify half of a number. This is an important step and shows that they are able to move from the concrete to the abstract.

### Next steps
● This activity should develop children's ability to generalise about the properties of odd and even numbers. It is important that they do not simply know and remember that only even numbers can be equally divided by two, but also understand why this is the case.
● Practical materials are an important aid for exploring and developing understanding in mathematics. This is true for all children, including the more able. A more able child may, however, choose to abandon concrete materials early in an activity. You should ensure that their reason for doing so is not because they consider the materials to be 'babyish' but because their understanding has developed sufficiently to work without them.
● There are other activities in this book which explore the properties of odd and even numbers; these include Lesson 46 (Domino sort) and Lesson 48 (Number sort).
● Making the link between halving and doubling is also important. As a further investigation, give the children the following task: Double the length of the snakes that could not be half covered in the activity. Can they now be half covered?

# Cover half

■ Cover half
of this snake
with cubes.

■ Create your own snake by colouring in 13 squares in the grid below.
■ Is it possible to cover half of your snake with cubes?
■ Increase the size of your snake. Can you cover half with cubes?

# Jump to 24

## Learning objectives

**(Y1) Use/apply strand:** Describe simple patterns and relationships involving numbers or shapes; decide whether examples satisfy given conditions.

**(Y1) Knowledge strand:** Count on or back in ones, twos, fives and tens.

**(Y2) Calculate strand:** Represent repeated addition and arrays as multiplication, and sharing and repeated subtraction (grouping) as division; use practical and informal written methods to support multiplication and division, including calculations with remainders.

## Expected prior knowledge

● Count in steps of different sizes.

## You will need

Enlarged version of the number track on photocopiable page 31; photocopiable page 31 (one per child); a small plastic toy to represent jumps along the number track (one per child).

## Key vocabulary

groups of, multiples of, factors of

## Activity introduction

● Display an enlarged version of the number track on photocopiable page 31.
● Ask: *If a toy jumped along the track in jumps of one, would it land on number 24? If it took jumps of two, would it still land on number 24?*
● Ask the children to investigate whether or not the toy will always land on number 24, whatever sized jump it takes.

## Activity development

● Give each child a copy of photocopiable page 31 together with a small toy and allow them to investigate the problem independently. Let them use the table on the sheet to record their answers.
● Once the children discover that some sized jumps result in a remainder, ask them to record this in the final column of the table.

## Review

● Bring the children back together and ask them to share their results. Record their solutions in a table on the whiteboard as shown below (the final column should be left blank to begin with).

| Jumps | Yes | No | Remainder | Number of jumps |
|---|---|---|---|---|
| 1 | ✓ | | | 24 |
| 2 | ✓ | | | 12 |
| 3 | ✓ | | | 8 |
| 4 | ✓ | | | 6 |
| 5 | | ✓ | 4 | |
| 6 | ✓ | | | 4 |
| 7 | | ✓ | 3 | |
| 8 | ✓ | | | 3 |
| 9 | | ✓ | 6 | |
| 10 | | ✓ | 4 | |
| 11 | | ✓ | 2 | |
| 12 | ✓ | | | 2 |
| 13 | | ✓ | 11 | |

● Ask: *How many jumps did the toy take to reach 24 when it jumped in twos?*
● Repeat the question for jumps of 3, 4, 6, 8, and 12 and record the answers in the table.
● Explain to the children that the sizes of jump that allowed the toy to land on 24 represent factors of 24: the numbers all divide exactly into 24 without a remainder.
● Investigating factors and multiples in this practical manner enables children to gain an understanding of multiplication and division. There is often confusion between the words 'factors' and 'multiples'. Multiple is linked with multiplication. 24 is a multiple of 6, since 6 can be multiplied a number of times (4 times) to total 24. Factor is linked with division. 6 is a factor of 24 since it will divide equally (4 times) into it.

### Next steps
● Ask the children to investigate factors of other numbers. Like 24, 36 has a high number of factors and is a good number to choose.

| 1 |
| 2 |
| 3 |
| 4 |
| 5 |
| 6 |
| 7 |
| 8 |
| 9 |
| 10 |
| 11 |
| 12 |
| 13 |
| 14 |
| 15 |
| 16 |
| 17 |
| 18 |
| 19 |
| 20 |
| 21 |
| 22 |
| 23 |
| 24 |

# Jump to 24

■ Can you take equal jumps to reach 24?

| Jumps | Yes | No | Remainder |
|---|---|---|---|
|  |  |  |  |
|  |  |  |  |
|  |  |  |  |
|  |  |  |  |
|  |  |  |  |
|  |  |  |  |
|  |  |  |  |
|  |  |  |  |
|  |  |  |  |
|  |  |  |  |
|  |  |  |  |

# Three-digit number

## Activity introduction

- Write the numbers 1 and 2 on the board. Ask: *Which numbers can be made using these digits?* Accept the answers 12 and 21.
- Repeat the activity with 1, 2 and 3. Establish that the answers are 123, 132, 213, 231, 312 and 321.
- Ask: *Which are the smallest and largest numbers that can be made with the digits 1, 2 and 3?* (123 and 321.) *What is the total of the three digits used in the numbers?* (6.) *Could any other three-digit number be made where the digits total 6?* (222, 411 or 330, or any variation on these.)

## Activity development

- Provide each child with photocopiable page 33 and a set of 0-9 number cards. Read through the problem on the sheet with the class. Encourage the children to use their number cards and move them around on the photocopiable page to investigate possible solutions. The first step is to find a group of three number cards with a total of 12. Solutions may be recorded on the sheet or a separate piece of paper.
- When the first group of three number cards has been exhausted (children should find all six different arrangements and then identify the smallest and largest number), challenge the children to find other possible solutions.
- Since there is a large number of solutions, it is unlikely that the children will find all of them in the time allowed. They may also find it difficult to be systematic in their selection and may at times work randomly.

## Solutions

- There are seven groups of three number cards with a total of 12: 3, 4, 5; 2, 4, 6; 1, 5, 6; 2, 3, 7; 8, 3, 1; 9, 2, 1; 9, 3, 0.
- 930 is the largest number overall and 156 is the smallest.

## Review

- Share solutions and encourage the children to explain how they know they have found the largest and smallest numbers.

---

### Learning objectives
**(Y1) Use/apply strand:**
Solve problems involving counting, adding, subtracting, doubling or halving in the context of numbers, measures or money.
**(Y2) Counting strand:** Read and write two-digit and three-digit numbers in figures and words.

### Expected prior knowledge
- Understand that the value of a digit is dependent on where it is placed in a number.

### You will need
Photocopiable page 33 (one per child); 0-9 number cards (one set per child).

### Key vocabulary
ones, tens, hundreds, digits

### Brainteaser link
18: 'How many numbers?' on page 17.

---

### Next steps

- A secure understanding of place value is essential for success in calculation. The following activity can be used repeatedly as a follow-up task.
- Children draw three boxes (as in the main activity above) and a 'bucket'.
- Randomly select a digit between 0 and 9. Children must write this digit in one of their three boxes or discard it into their bucket.
- The aim is to make the largest number possible. Once a number has been positioned it cannot be changed.
- This activity provides an opportunity to use the strategies developed above by aiming to place the largest digit in the hundreds position and the smallest in the ones position. There is, however, an element of luck involved as there is no guarantee which digits will be selected.

# Three-digit number

Sally has made a three-digit number using numbers between 0 and 9. The total of the three digits is 12.

◼ Which numbers could she have made? Write them here:

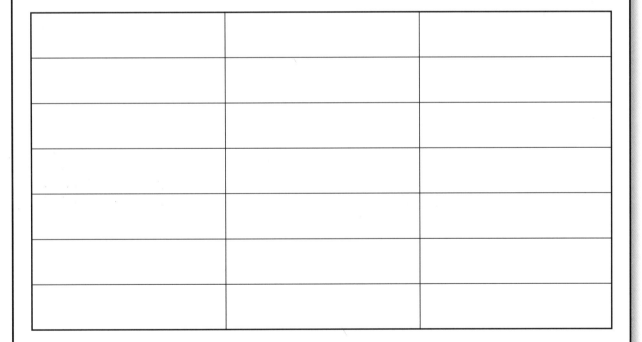

| | | |
|---|---|---|
| | | |
| | | |
| | | |
| | | |
| | | |
| | | |

◼ Which is the largest number? _____

◼ Which is the smallest number? _____

# LESSON 4

# The broken necklace

## Learning objectives
**(Y1) Use/apply strand:** Describe ways of solving puzzles and problems, explaining choices and decisions orally or using pictures.
**(Y2) Use/apply strand:** Describe patterns and relationships involving numbers or shapes.
**(Y2) Use/apply strand:** Present solutions to puzzles and problems in an organised way.

## Expected prior knowledge
● Understand a pattern as a relationship between colours or objects.

## You will need
A collection of red, green and blue beads and threading strings (interlocking cubes may be used as an alternative); photocopiable page 35 (one per child); colouring pens or pencils (one red, one green and one blue pen/pencil per child).

## Key vocabulary
describe the pattern, beside, next to

## Brainteaser link
6: 'Crack the code' on page 13.

## Activity introduction
● Ask: *What comes next in the sequence red, blue, red, blue? What comes next in the sequence red, red, blue, red, red, blue?* Take responses and establish that the children understand what a sequence is.
● Show some beads or interlocking cubes and ask the children to work in pairs to create their own sequence.
● Ask each pair to share their sequence with the rest of the group and ask what comes next.

## Activity development
● Provide each child with photocopiable page 35 and a threading string, beads or interlocking cubes (eight red, eight green and eight blue).
● Ask: *What has happened to Princess Pat's necklace?* Establish that the jewels of her necklace need to be put back together in a sequence. Ask the children to find as many ways as possible to do this.
● Explain that the children should create a suitable sequence, using all the beads or cubes you have given them to try out their ideas.
● The solutions should then be recorded by colouring the sets of beads on the photocopiable sheet. Some solutions are shown below.

## Solutions
R = Ruby (red), E = Emerald (green), S = Sapphire (blue)

## Review
● Ask the children to share their solutions. They may produce alternative solutions where there is an attempt at a sequence, but the pattern is not maintained or does not use all of the jewels. Allow them to explain their sequence and acknowledge where they have produced a pattern. Often there is more than one answer to the question of what comes next.
● Encourage recognition of similarities between solutions. For example: R, E, S, R, E, S is similar to S, E, R, S, E, R. The difference is that the order is reversed.

## Next steps
● Sequences and patterns are intertwined. A sequence is a set of numbers or objects, made and written in order according to some mathematical rule. Within mathematics, pattern has a similar meaning. There are many different types of pattern but repetition in some way underlies all patterns.
● Encourage children to recognise pattern in the environment; for example floor tiles, wrapping paper, wheel trims on cars.
● Recognition of pattern within number is also important. A good activity is to look for pattern in the times-tables. All tables have some pattern. For example, the 5 times-table has a 5, 0, 5, 0 pattern for the last digit. An odd-numbered table has an odd, even, odd, even pattern.

34

50 MATHS LESSONS FOR MORE ABLE LEARNERS · AGES 5-7

Name _____

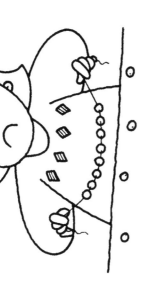

# The broken necklace

■ Princess Pat's necklace is broken. Help her put it back together.

■ The necklace has:
  8 red rubies
  8 green emeralds
  8 blue sapphires.

■ Arrange the jewels so that they form a pattern.

■ How many ways can you do it?

■ Record your results here.

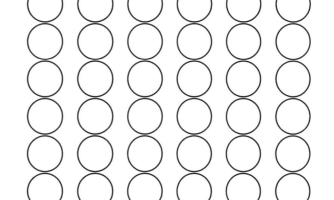

Illustration © Gaynor Berry

# Number grids

## Activity introduction
- Write a number sequence on the board (for example: 5, 10, 15, 20). Ask: *What number comes next in this sequence?*
- Repeat the activity with two more sequences (for example: 12, 15, 18 and 120, 130, 140). Ask: *How do you know which number comes next?*
- Ask a volunteer to create their own number sequence and write it on the board. Can the rest of the group identify which number comes next?
- Repeat for other number sequences.

## Activity development
- Provide each child with photocopiable page 37 and explain that the numbers in the grids form part of a sequence; the children have to fill in the missing numbers. Allow them to work independently.
- Explain that the grid with only one number in it and the blank grids are for the children to create their own sequences for others to solve. Remind them that they will need to put at least two numbers into the grid in order for others to work out the number sequence.

## Solutions

| 2 | 3 | 4 |
|---|---|---|
| 5 | 6 | 7 |
| 8 | 9 | 10 |

| 5 | 10 | 15 |
|---|---|---|
| 20 | 25 | 30 |
| 35 | 40 | 45 |

| 100 | 101 | 102 |
|---|---|---|
| 103 | 104 | 105 |
| 106 | 107 | 108 |

| 41 | 43 | 45 |
|---|---|---|
| 47 | 49 | 51 |
| 53 | 55 | 57 |

| 0 | 3 | 6 |
|---|---|---|
| 9 | 12 | 15 |
| 18 | 21 | 24 |

| a | c | e |
|---|---|---|
| g | i | k |
| m | o | q |

| 490 | 500 | 510 |
|---|---|---|
| 520 | 530 | 540 |
| 550 | 560 | 570 |

## Review
- Share solutions to the set number sequences.
- Encourage the children to look at other patterns in the number grids.
- Ask: *Is there a sequence if we read down the columns rather than across the rows?* For example, on the first grid 2, 5, 8 goes up in 3s. On the second grid, 5, 20, 35 goes up in 15s.
- Ask the children to present their own sequences for others to solve.

### Next steps
- Recognition of pattern and sequences is important for later work in algebra.
- A strategy for the recognition of sequences is first to count and make a note of the differences between consecutive numbers, and then look to see if there is a pattern between these differences. The difference may not be the same each time but there may be a pattern (for example, the difference may increase by one each time, as in 3, 4, 6, 9, 13…).
- Children should be exposed to a variety of types of sequences, including those that increase, decrease and develop in different-sized steps.

Name _____

# Number grids

■ Fill in the missing numbers on the number grids below. The last five grids can be used to create your own sequences.

| 2 |  |  |
|---|---|---|
|  |  |  |
|  |  | 10 |

| 5 | 10 |  |
|---|---|---|
|  |  |  |
|  | 40 |  |

|  | 101 |  |
|---|---|---|
| 103 | 104 |  |
|  |  |  |

| 41 |  | 45 |
|---|---|---|
|  | 51 |  |
|  | 57 |  |

|  |  |  |
|---|---|---|
|  | 12 | 15 |
| 18 |  |  |

| a | c |  |
|---|---|---|
|  |  | k |
|  | o |  |

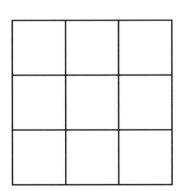

| 490 | 500 |  |
|---|---|---|
|  | 530 |  |
|  | 560 |  |

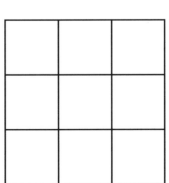

|  |  |  |
|---|---|---|
|  | 20 |  |
|  |  |  |

|  |  |  |
|---|---|---|
|  |  |  |
|  |  |  |

|  |  |  |
|---|---|---|
|  |  |  |
|  |  |  |

|  |  |  |
|---|---|---|
|  |  |  |
|  |  |  |

|  |  |  |
|---|---|---|
|  |  |  |
|  |  |  |

# Which pizza is whose?

## Learning objectives

**(Y1) Use/apply strand:**
Describe ways of solving puzzles and problems, explaining choices and decisions orally or using pictures.

**(Y2) Use/apply strand:**
Follow a line of enquiry; answer questions by choosing and using suitable equipment and selecting, organising and presenting information in lists, tables and simple diagrams.

**(Y2) Counting strand:** Find one half, one quarter and three quarters of shapes and sets of objects.

**(Y3) Use/apply strand:**
Follow a line of enquiry by deciding what information is important; make and use lists, tables and graphs to organise and interpret the information.

## Expected prior knowledge

● Read and work in a group.
● Use logical thinking to sort information.

## You will need

Interactive whiteboard (or ordinary whiteboard); photocopiable page 39 (one per group of up to four children); blank version of photocopiable page 39 (one per group).

## Key vocabulary

sections, equal, half, fourths, twice as many, information, relevant, systematic, sorting, reason, justify

## Brainteaser links

8: 'Is it true?' on page 13.
14: 'Football kit' on page 15.

## Activity introduction

● On an interactive whiteboard (or ordinary whiteboard), draw four pizzas (three divided into six sections and one divided into eight sections). Draw tomato slices and cheese chunks on the sections, as follows (or you can make up your own combinations and questions).

Pizza 1: Four of six sections have cheese chunks (two on two sections, and three on two sections).

Pizza 2: Two sections of six have cheese chunks and tomato slices (three cheese chunks and three tomato slices).

Pizza 3: Four sections of six have both cheese chunks and tomato slices.

Pizza 4: Six of eight sections have cheese chunks only.

● Set the following scenario: *A family went to the pizza restaurant for lunch. They all ordered different combinations. Can you work out which pizza belongs to each person?*

a) *Mum's pizza had an equal number of cheese chunks and tomato slices. Which one could be Mum's pizza?* Discuss and question the children's justifications.

b) *On Dad's pizza one third of the slices have toppings. Which one could be Dad's pizza?*

c) *Zak's pizza is cut into sixths. Which one could Zak's pizza be?*

d) *Kerry hates tomatoes. Which is her pizza?*

● Give the children time to think the problem through before gathering their answers. Does everyone agree? Discuss the children's justifications for their answers.

## Activity development

● Provide each group of up to four children with photocopiable page 39. (If you wish, you can copy the four clues onto card and laminate them so that they can be used again.)

● Introduce the idea of working as a collaborative group, as in the introductory task. Make sure each group understands that they might not be able to solve the problem straight away.

## Solution

A Matthew
B Nadia
C Caleb
D Jessica

## Review

● Review the vocabulary and relate its meaning to what the children were doing.

## Next steps

● Ask each group to make up their own 'Which pizza is whose?' puzzle for another group to solve. Provide blank versions of photocopiable page 39 so that they can write their own clues and add their own toppings to the pizzas.

Name _____

# Which pizza is whose?

A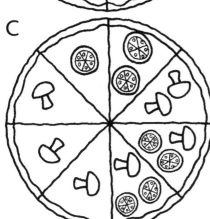

B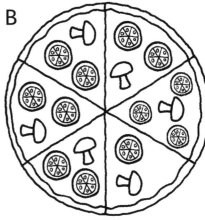

🍄 = mushroom

🍅 = tomato

C

D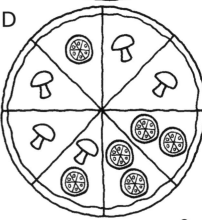

---

Caleb's pizza has tomatoes on half of its slices.
◼ Find Caleb's pizza.

Caleb _____

Jessica's pizza was cut into fourths, but she cut each slice in half because the pieces were too big to eat.
◼ Find Jessica's pizza.

Jessica _____

Matthew's pizza has twice as many mushrooms as Jessica's pizza.
◼ Find Matthew's pizza.

Matthew _____

The four children can equally share the tomatoes on Nadia's pizza, but they cannot share the mushrooms equally.
◼ Find Nadia's pizza.

Nadia _____

Illustration © Gaynor Berry

# Between and difference between

## Learning objectives
**(Y1) Use/apply strand:**
Solve problems involving counting, adding [and] subtracting in the context of numbers.
**(Y1) Counting strand:**
Compare and order numbers, using the related vocabulary.
**(Y2) Use/apply strand:**
Solve problems involving addition [and] subtraction.
**(Y2) Counting strand:**
Order two-digit numbers and position them on a number line.

## Expected prior knowledge
● Recognise place value of numbers up to and including 20.
● Use the terms 'between' and 'difference' (and other vocabulary related to subtraction).

## You will need
Photocopiable page 41 (one per pair); 1–20 number cards (one set per pair); pencils and paper.

## Key vocabulary
between, difference between, calculate, subtract, take away

## Brainteaser links
7: 'What's my rule?' on page 13.
10: 'The answer is...' on page 14.

## Activity introduction
● Give each pair of children a copy of photocopiable page 41 and a set of 1–20 number cards (shuffled and laid in a pile face down). The instructions for the game are given on the photocopiable page.

## Activity development
● When the children have used all their cards they must look back at their answers and discuss any pattern they see: they should notice that the number of cards between any two is always one less by one than the difference between the two. Ask the children to think about why this is and tell them you will ask them to explain their thoughts in the Review session.
● The children could use a larger pack of numbers (for example, a pack of 1–50 number cards) or a different range (for example, 21–50). This activity will help them to become familiar with two-digit numbers and develop their thinking and knowledge of the number system.
● If any of the children are struggling, a number line or 100-square could be used to support their thinking.

## Review
● Gather the children's thoughts about why the number of cards between any two is always one less by one than the difference between the two. Reinforce their understanding of what the difference between two numbers is.

### Next steps
● A set of larger numbers could be used.
● Review the vocabulary specific to the activity (see 'Key vocabulary' left).

Name _____

# Between and difference between

■ Shuffle a pack of cards numbered from 1–20.

■ Take two cards from the pack.

■ Ask your partner to place them in order (smallest to largest).

■ Ask your partner to write down the numbers between the two cards. For example, if you pick 4 and 11, your partner writes down 5, 6, 7, 8, 9 and 10.

■ Ask how many numbers there are. For 4 and 11, the answer is 6.

■ Ask your partner what the difference between the numbers is. For 4 and 11, the difference is 7. (4 – 11 = 7)

■ Is your partner correct? If they got one question correct they keep one card (it doesn't matter which). The other card goes to the bottom of the pack. If they got both questions correct they keep both cards.

■ Your partner then takes two cards and asks you the same two questions.

■ Continue until all the cards are taken. Count up how many cards you each have. The winner is the one with the most cards.

Illustration © Gaynor Berry

# Petra's pet shop

## Learning objectives

**(Y1) Use/apply strand:**
Describe ways of solving puzzles and problems, explaining choices and decisions orally or using pictures.
**(Y2) Use/apply strand:**
Follow a line of enquiry; answer questions by choosing and using suitable equipment and selecting, organising and presenting information in lists, tables and simple diagrams.

## Expected prior knowledge
- Read and work in a group.
- Use logical thinking to sort information.

## You will need
Interactive whiteboard (optional); prepared set of 'pet shops' and clue cards from photocopiable page 43, enlarged and laminated (one per group of four children); blank set of 'pet shops' and clue cards.

## Key vocabulary
information, relevant, systematic, sorting, reason, justify

## Brainteaser link
8: 'Is it true?' on page 13.

## Activity introduction
- On an interactive whiteboard (or ordinary whiteboard), draw three pet shops (similar to those on photocopiable page 43) with a variety of pets in five of the six sections; use the sixth for a door. For example:
  Shop 1: Rectory Farm pet shop has 2 rabbits, 2 gerbils and 1 hamster.
  Shop 2: Barry Road pet shop has 2 gerbils, 1 hamster, 1 rabbit and 1 snake.
  Shop 3: The Green pet shop has 2 rabbits, 1 gerbil, 1 hamster and 1 snake.
- Write these clues (or similar) on the board:
  Sasha's favourite pet shop has 2 rabbits.
  Sasha's favourite pet shop has 1 snake.
  Sasha's favourite pet shop has 1 hamster.
  Sasha's favourite pet shop has 1 gerbil.
- Ask: *Which is Sasha's favourite pet shop?*
- Give the children some time to think the statements through and discuss their ideas with a partner before deciding on their answers.
- Gather the answers. Who agrees/disagrees? Discuss the children's justifications for their answers.

## Activity development
- Provide each group with a prepared set of 'pet shops' and clue cards from photocopiable page 43.
- Introduce the idea of working as a collaborative group, as modelled in the introduction, and make sure that each group understands their task (to find out which is Petra's pet shop) and realises that the problem might not be solved straight away.
- Each child takes one clue card and reads it aloud to the group. In order to ensure that there is a collaborative discussion, with no dominant character taking over the activity, each child should hold on to their card and not show it to the others.

## Solution
- Shop D.

## Review
- Review the vocabulary (see 'Key vocabulary' left) and relate its meaning to what the children were doing.

### Next steps
- Children make up their own puzzle for another group to solve. Provide blank cards for them to write their clues on and blank grids for them to add their pets.

# Petra's pet shop

A

B

C

D

E

F

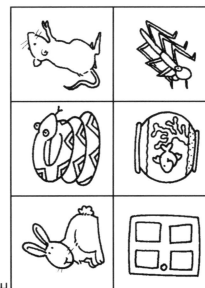

Petra's pet shop has
2 fish

Petra's pet shop has
1 rabbit

Petra's pet shop has
1 stick insect

Petra's pet shop has
1 snake

Illustration © Gaynor Berry

# Find the missing domino

## Activity introduction

- This initial activity just involves the seven double dominoes. Prepare a large display set in which one of the doubles is missing (for example, double 4). Place these display doubles randomly on the class whiteboard, or on an interactive whiteboard. Ask: *Which double is missing?* Ask the children how they came to their answer. Encourage the arrangement to an ordered orientation to help them to 'see' the answer.
- Hand out photocopiable page 45 and sets of dominoes. Look at the table. Explain that in their pairs/groups the children need to find all the dominoes with a pattern of five dots on them. Collect ideas on how they might do that.
- When they think they have found them all, ask them to say how they 'know' they have found them all.
- Collect their ideas of how they found their answers.

## Activity development

- Before introducing the following activity, remove one piece with a '3' on it out of each set of dominoes. Place the removed pieces in separate envelopes.
- Now ask the children to find all the dominoes with three dots on them (as you have hidden one to see if you can trick them). Ask them to think about how they might identify the missing domino easily and record this on their sheets.
- Ask the following questions: *Did you use the strategies discussed earlier, or did you use new strategies? Which strategies are most effective?*
- Hand out an envelope to each pair/group. Ask the children to lay out their dominoes on the tables and mix them up (see extension activity on page 45). Take one domino away from the set (without looking at it!) and place it in their envelopes. Can the children find the missing domino by sorting the other dominoes in order?
- As an alternative activity, ask each pair or group to swap sets that have had a domino already removed. Can the children find the other group or pair's missing domino?

## Review

- Ask: *What were the most effective strategies you used to find missing dominoes?* Gather the children's ideas or ask them to present the way in which the pairs or groups organised their dominoes to find the missing piece.

### Learning objectives
**(Y1) Use/apply strand:**
Describe ways of solving puzzles and problems, explaining choices and decisions orally or using pictures.
**(Y1) Counting strand:**
Compare and order numbers, using the related vocabulary.
**(Y2) Use/apply strand:**
Describe patterns and relationships involving numbers or shapes.

### Expected prior knowledge
- Familiarity with a set of dominoes (but not essential).

### You will need
Photocopiable page 45 (one per pair); a set of dominoes (one per pair/small group); envelopes.

### Key vocabulary
organise, strategy, efficient, quickest, set, group/family

### Brainteaser link
11: 'How many words?' on page 14.

### Next steps
- To extend this idea, one child could take a domino and the other(s) have to find out which one it is. Alternatively, take more than one domino away without looking at them. Can the children identify the missing pieces?
- If the children are not familiar with dominoes, ask them to lay out the dominoes to match their ends. Can they join them up into a loop with no gaps? What strategies did they use to help them achieve this?

Name _____

# Find the missing domino

## Recording table

| Investigate | Complete the domino set (draw in the dots) How will you order them? | | | | | | | |
|---|---|---|---|---|---|---|---|---|
| How many dominoes have five dots on them? | | | | | | | | |
| Find all the dominoes with three dots on them. Now work out which domino is missing. | | | | | | | | |
| How many dominoes have three dots on them? | | | | | | | | |

## Extension

■ Using a whole set of dominoes, lay out the pieces face down. Without looking, remove one and place it in an envelope. Hand this envelope to your teacher. Remember to think about how you can find the missing piece so that you can present your ideas to the group.

# Making money

## Learning objectives
**(Y1) Use/apply strand:** Solve problems involving counting, adding, subtracting, doubling or halving in the context of numbers, measures or money.
**(Y2) Use/apply strand:** Solve problems involving addition, subtraction, multiplication or division in contexts of numbers, measures or pounds and pence.
**(Y3) Counting strand:** Partition three-digit numbers into multiples of 100, 10 and 1 in different ways.
**(Y4) Counting strand:** Use decimal notation for tenths and hundredths and partition decimals; relate the notation to money.

## Expected prior knowledge
● Recognition that 1p is the same as £0.01 and 10p is the same as £0.10, and that there are 100 pence in one pound.

## You will need
Dice (one ordinary and one showing £0.10, £0.10, £0.10, £0.01, £0.01, £0.01 per pair); plenty of 1p, 2p, 5p, 10p, 20p, 50p and a few one pound and two pound coins (one set per pair); photocopiable page 47 (one per child).

## Key vocabulary
pence, value, total, equivalent values, decimal/money notation

## Brainteaser links
2: 'The last penny' on page 11.
4: 'Find the magic number' on page 12.

## Activity introduction
● Begin by ensuring that the children understand the game on photocopiable page 47.
● Working with a partner, the children take it in turns to throw the two dice (or throw one each). The dice tell the children how much money they can collect from their bank. For example: if they throw a 5 and £0.01, they can collect 5 pennies (or the equivalent) from the bank.
● The children continue like this until they have had ten goes. They then add up the total of their money and write it down. They must try to express it as a decimal figure (for example, £2.43).
● You may want to demonstrate this before setting the children to work independently. Useful questions to ask during the demonstration are: *Can you tell me what the two dice say? How much money should I take? I've got lots of pennies here; can I exchange them to help me add them up? What could I exchange my pennies for? How much money have I got altogether? How do I write down this total? Is there another way?*

## Activity development
● Children could work separately to see who in each pair can collect the most money.
● The table on photocopiable page 47 can be used to record the money collected.
● If you choose to make the game a little longer, you might want to consider the use of calculators to help the children keep a running total.
● When the children feel confident enough to work independently on this game it will provide you with the opportunity to assess their understanding of money notation and the way in which they count and organise their money. For example, can they make appropriate exchanges of amounts (such as ten 1p coins for a 10p piece)? Can they write down amounts of money correctly? Can they use the zero (place value) correctly?

## Review
● Review the different totals achieved and ask appropriate questions.
● Talk about any difficulties or confusions the pairs encountered, particularly when exchanging coins for equivalent values.

### Next steps
● A third dice could be used with + and – (make sure you have more plus symbols than minus as the game could produce a negative amount). The children then carry out the appropriate addition or subtraction using the amounts thrown on the dice.
● Review the vocabulary specific to the activity (see 'Key vocabulary' left).

# Making money

| £ | 10p | 1p |
|---|-----|-----|
|   |     |     |

# Busy bees

## Learning objectives
**(Y1) Use/apply strand:**
Solve problems involving counting... in the context of numbers.
**(Y1) Counting strand:**
Compare and order numbers, using the related vocabulary.
**(Y2) Use/apply strand:**
Describe patterns and relationships involving numbers or shapes; make predictions and test these with examples.
**(Y2) Counting strand:**
Order two-digit numbers and position them on a number line.

## Expected prior knowledge
● Order numbers up to and including 20.
● Use the vocabulary of ordinal numbers.

## You will need
Laminated sheet of flowers and bees (see activity introduction); photocopiable page 49 (one per child/pair).

## Key vocabulary
ordinal numbers, 1st, 2nd, 3rd..., first, second, third...

## Brainteaser link
6: 'Crack the code' on page 13.

## Activity introduction
● Using clipart or other illustrations, prepare a large sheet of paper showing 10–20 colourful flowers (and laminate if possible). Prepare and laminate seven bees (Boris and his friends) for the children to move around the flowers; doing this will extend the concept of ordinal numbers and develop children's ability to ask further questions.
● As an introduction to the main activity, use an interactive whiteboard to present a simpler problem. For example, draw five flowers with two of the flowers showing bees gathering pollen. Ask: *Which flowers could the next bee land on if bees are already on some flowers?*
● Discuss the ordinal names of numbers. This could be developed by adding another five flowers to your row on the board and adding three more bees. Ask the same question. Discuss the children's understanding of ordinal vocabulary.
● Hand out copies of photocopiable page 49. Working with a partner (or independently), children answer the questions on the sheet.
● When they have answered the first three questions, there is an extension question involving 18 flowers. Ask the children to place six bees on any flowers. They should then ask a friend to work out where Boris can land (tell them to work out the answer themselves before asking their friend).

## Activity development
● When the children have completed page 49, you can develop these ideas in a variety of ways. The 'Next steps' section below offers you one idea but, depending on the progress children have made, you could offer a more complicated question, asking about pairs of numbers (for example, the first pair, the second pair, and so on). The context of a row of flowers could be continued through choosing bunches of flowers; changing the story, Boris could choose the third pair, fourth pair (and so on) or the second bunch, third bunch, tenth bunch (and so on). This will provide the opportunity for you to assess the children's understanding of ordinal sets of numbers.

## Review
● Gather the children's answers and talk about the questions they set for their friends. Discuss any problems or difficulties that may have arisen. Invite the children to think of other questions they could ask their friends regarding ordinal numbers.

### Next steps
● This activity can be used in other contexts (for example, children choosing cars or horses on a fairground ride). Suitable resources could be made to take the ideas further. For example, to develop the understanding of multiples of 10, you could use bunches of ten flowers in different pots, or you could construct a model merry-go-round where every tenth horse is blue.

LESSON 11

Name _____

# Busy bees

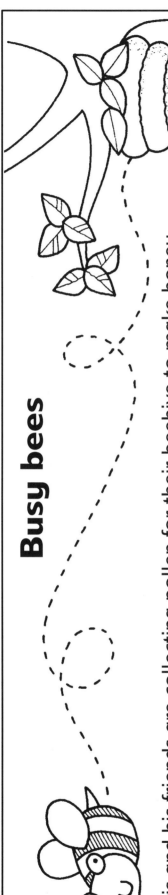

Boris and his friends are collecting pollen for their beehive to make honey. They come across a row of flowers. Bella, Betty, Banjit, Brian, Beski and Barney fly straight to the 2nd, 4th, 5th, 7th, 9th and 11th flowers in the row.

■ Which flowers could Boris fly to?

1  2  3  4  5  6  7  8  9  10  11  12

■ Which flowers could Boris fly to if his friends were collecting pollen from:
a) the second, fourth, fifth, seventh, eighth, and twelfth flowers?
b) the 1st, 2nd, 4th, 5th, 7th and 8th flowers?

## Extension

■ What if there were 18 flowers in the row? Decide which flowers Boris' six friends might land on, then ask a friend which flowers Boris could land on.

Illustration © Gaynor Berry

# Marbles in pockets

## Learning objectives
(Y1) Use/apply strand:
Solve problems involving counting, adding, subtracting, doubling or halving in the context of numbers.
(Y2) Use/apply strand:
Present solutions to puzzles and problems in an organised way.
(Y2) Knowledge strand:
Derive and recall all addition and subtraction facts for each number to at least 10, all pairs with totals to 20.

## Expected prior knowledge
● Display knowledge of number bonds to 10.

## You will need
Photocopiable page 51 (one per child); marbles or other objects for counting; two pots or plates to represent two pockets.

## Key vocabulary
how many ways, count, total

## Brainteaser links
1: 'In the bag' on page 11.
12: 'Number bond suits' on page 15.

## Activity introduction
● Revise the children's understanding of number bonds to 10 by asking: *How many ways can we make 10?* List the possible answers on the board (for example, 1 + 9 = 10, 3 + 7 = 10 and so on). Ask: *Have we got them all? How can we check?*
● Support the children in arranging the bonds systematically in order to check that they are all there (0,10; 1,9; 2,8; 3,7; 4,6; 5,5; 6,4; 7,3; 8,2; 9,1; 10,0).

## Activity development
● Hand out copies of photocopiable page 51 and explain the problem to the children. Provide them with marbles and 'pockets' so that they can work practically when tackling the activity.
● Encourage the children to work independently on the activity. Remind them of the method of working systematically, but do not force them to do so.
● Encourage them to use the available practical materials to begin with, although some may not need them.
● Allow them to record their solutions in their own way, or to use the table on the photocopiable page if they prefer. For those who finish quickly, ask: *What would happen if Joe had 30/50/100 marbles?*

## Review
● Share the children's solutions and methods of recording. Draw particular attention to those who recorded their answers systematically and show how easy it is to check that they have found all the possible solutions. Highlight the link between number bonds to 10 and 20. For example: 8 + 2 = 10; 18 + 2 = 20.
● Ask: *What would happen if Joe had 1000 marbles and very large pockets? How many marbles could he put in each pocket?*
● Share some solutions on the board and encourage the children to make the link between number bonds to 10, 100 and 1000. For example: 8 + 2 = 10; 80 + 20 = 100; 800 + 200 = 1000.
● It is important that children have instant recall of number bonds, but also understand the relationship between them. This will also help them to derive facts. They should be encouraged to look for relationships and have the opportunity to explain them.

## Next steps
● Give children the opportunity to explore number bonds including 20 and 100. A bead bar or string is a useful resource. For example, one with 100 beads can be used to explore number bonds to 100 where the beads are divided into sections.

# Marbles in pockets

Joe has 20 marbles. He puts some in each of his two pockets.

◼ How many different ways can he do this?

◼ Use the table below to record your work.

| Pocket 1 | Pocket 2 |
|---|---|
|  |  |
|  |  |
|  |  |
|  |  |
|  |  |
|  |  |
|  |  |
|  |  |
|  |  |
|  |  |
|  |  |
|  |  |

Illustration © Gaynor Berry

# Multi-pairs

## Activity introduction
● Ask: *How can we find out how many groups of 4 there are in 24?* If the children already know the answer to this question, still get them to check.
● Show 24 cubes. Ask the children to take out groups of 4 and count how many there are. Establish that there are six groups of 4 in 24.
● Ask: *What will happen if we put pairs of 4 together?* (Establish that the answer is groups of 8.) How many groups of 8 are there in 24? (Establish that the answer is 3.) Ask: *If there are six groups of 4 in 24, how does that help us to work out how many groups of 8 there are?*

## Activity development
● Introduce photocopiable page 53. Ask the children to find pairs that give the same total. The obvious ones are those that demonstrate commutativity (for example, four groups of 3 and three groups of 4).
● Once the children have found these, ask: *Can you pair them in any other way?* Make reference to the activity above to stimulate thought.

## Review
● Create a table on the board (similar to that below) and ask the children to come out and write a statement in the correct square.
● Ask: *Are there any other calculations that could be added to the chart* (16 groups of 1). Introduce the word 'equivalent', explaining to the children that it means 'the same as'. Ask: *Do you know any other equivalent number sentences?* Record and discuss their suggestions.

| Totals of 6 | Totals of 12 | Totals of 16 | Totals of 20 |
|---|---|---|---|
| 1 group of 6 | 2 groups of 6 | 4 groups of 4 | 4 groups of 5 |
| 6 groups of 1 | 6 groups of 2 | 2 groups of 8 | 5 groups of 4 |
| 3 groups of 2 | 3 groups of 4 | 8 groups of 2 | 2 groups of 10 |
| 2 groups of 3 | 4 groups of 3 | 1 group of 16 | 10 groups of 2 |
| | 12 groups of 1 | | |
| | 1 group of 12 | | |

● The above matches represent equivalent calculations. Equivalence is an important idea in mathematics and opportunities for children to make connections between equivalents are valuable.

**Next steps**
● Extend the activity, using higher totals (for example, 30, 32, 36). Encourage the children to write equivalent number sentences for each total.

Name _____

# Multi-pairs

| | | |
|---|---|---|
| 4 groups of 4 | 2 groups of 3 | 8 groups of 2 |
| 1 group of 6 | 4 groups of 5 | 1 group of 12 |
| 12 groups of 1 | 2 groups of 8 | 2 groups of 6 |
| 3 groups of 2 | 3 groups of 4 | 6 groups of 1 |
| 5 groups of 4 | 10 groups of 2 | 1 group of 16 |
| 4 groups of 3 | 6 groups of 2 | 2 groups of 10 |

# More or less than 500?

## Learning objectives
**(Y2) Knowledge strand:**
Derive and recall all addition and subtraction facts for each number to at least 10, all pairs with totals to 20 and all pairs of multiples of 10 with totals up to 100.
**(Y3) Counting strand:**
Round two-digit or three-digit numbers to the nearest 10 or 100 and give estimates for their sums and differences.

## Expected prior knowledge
● Read three-digit numbers.
● Recall number bonds to 10 and 100.
● Partition numbers into hundreds, tens and ones.

## You will need
Photocopiable page 55 (one per child/pair); scissors (one pair per child/pair).

## Key vocabulary
more than, less than, estimate

## Brainteaser links
1: 'In the bag' on page 11.
3: 'Make 12' on page 12.
12: 'Number bond suits' on page 15.
17: 'How many?' on page 17.

## Activity introduction
● Revise number bonds to 10 and then to 100 and beyond.
● Ask questions such as: *What number do I need to add to 6 to make 10? What number do I need to add to 60 to make 100? What is 60 add 40? What is 100 add 100? What is 200 add 300? If I have 450, how many more do I need to make 500?*

## Activity development
● Provide the children with photocopiable page 55. Get the children to work in pairs as this encourages and supports discussion. Ideally, the number cards should be cut out from the sheet so that they can be moved around and paired up in different ways to complete the activity.
● As the children work together, ask: *If you choose 310, approximately how many more do you need to make 500? Does partitioning the number help? How can you use your knowledge of number bonds to 100 to support the calculations? Now that you have found two pairs of cards that total less than 500, can you find another pair? Using two cards, what is the highest/lowest total you can make?*
● Encourage the use of jottings to support calculation. For example:
　　260 + 240
　　Work out 200 + 200, jot down 400
　　Work out 40 + 60, jot down 100
　　The answer is 500.
● Encourage estimation where precise calculation is not required. For example, 150 + 180 is clearly less than 500 because both numbers are less than 200, and 200 + 200 = 400. A calculator can be used as a checking tool once an estimate has been made.
● Children work with large numbers in this activity, but these numbers are all multiples of 10. Place value and an appreciation of the size of the numbers will support calculation. The challenging element is bridging through 100.

## Solutions
● Totals of 500: 240 and 260; 320 and 180; 130 and 370; 150 and 350; 190 and 310.
● Pairs of more than 500: 320 and 260; 370 and 240; 350 and 180 (other combinations are possible).
● Pairs of less than 500: 260 and 130; 240 and 150; 190 and 180 (other combinations are possible).

## Review
● Share solutions and ask the children to discuss the strategies they used.
● Also share and model the use of jottings.

### Next steps
● More able learners often enjoy working with larger numbers. An application of place value can enable them to do so, particularly if the numbers are multiples of 10.
● A useful activity is to count in tens or hundreds beyond 100 or 1000.

# More or less than 500?

- ◼ Pair up these cards so that each pair totals 500.
- ◼ Re-arrange the cards and find two pairs of cards that total more than 500.
- ◼ Re-arrange the cards and find two pairs of cards that total less than 500.

| 240 | 350 |
|-----|-----|
| 150 | 190 |
| 130 | 260 |
| 320 | 310 |
| 370 | 180 |

# Fraction necklace

## Activity introduction

### Learning objectives
**(Y2) Use/apply strand:** Describe patterns and relationships involving numbers or shapes, make predictions and test these with examples.
**(Y2) Counting strand:** Find one half, one quarter and three quarters of shapes and sets of objects.
**(Y3) Use/apply strand:** Describe and explain methods, choices and solutions to puzzles and problems, orally and in writing, using pictures and diagrams.

### Expected prior knowledge
● Be able to describe and continue repeating patterns.

### You will need
Plastic links or linking cubes; photocopiable page 57 (one per pair); number lines; 100-squares.

### Key vocabulary
fractions, whole, part, equal parts, thirds, quarters, halves, half, divide, groups

### Brainteaser link
6: 'Crack the code' on page 13.

● This activity further develops children's understanding of place value, halving, fractions as part of a whole and dividing odd and even numbers in half. It also encourages them to begin to think about other fractions such as thirds, quarters and eighths.
● Provide the children with a collection of plastic links or linking cubes. Begin by linking together a collection of two colours of links (for example, link blue and red links (r,r,r,r,r,r,b,b,b,b,b) alternately: r,b,r,b,r,b,r,b,r,b,r. Make sure they have an even total of links.
● Ask questions: *Can you identify if you have an even number of colours? How can you check? Can you make your necklace into two halves (one of each colour)? If you can't, what can you do?* (Swap some of your links so that you have an even number of colours.) *Can you split the half necklace in half again?* (Some will not split evenly again, depending on the number of links they have.) Discuss this point with the children, why some will/will not.
● Introduce quarters. Encourage the children to identify how many links there are in the whole necklace, half of the necklace and a quarter of the necklace.
● Ask related questions, this time about quarters and, if appropriate, introduce eighths (as half of a quarter). If the children are not yet ready for this development, discuss the different lengths when the necklace is split in half. Ask: *If the two halves have the same number of links, there are two equal lengths. How many other equal lengths can you make out of your necklace? Can you make three equal lengths? What about four equal lengths?*
● Discuss how many equal parts you can divide your necklace into and help the children to connect the relationship between equal parts and fraction vocabulary.

## Activity development
● Hand out copies of photocopiable page 57. Invite the children to use the table on this sheet to record the fraction necklaces they made.
● Some children could investigate systematically by using lengths of 2 up to 10 or 20. Ask which lengths can be halved and which cannot.
● Produce a table showing the number of links in a 'whole' necklace they have made.

## Review
● Ask individuals what lengths of necklace they investigated. Gather information on the board for all to see. Discuss as a group any patterns or relationships discovered in the investigation. Were there any lengths of necklace which would not divide at all?

### Next steps
● Provide further plastic links for the children to investigate longer necklaces. Ask them to divide up their necklaces into thirds and guide them in using their knowledge of times tables. This can be extended for some children to think about other fractions, such as sixths and eighths, and their relationship with thirds and quarters and halves.

# Fraction necklace

● Record your necklace. Use coloured pens or pencils to help your thinking.

● Discuss how you might record your groupings of links.

| Whole necklace | Half necklace (halves) | Half of a half necklace (quarters) | Half of a half of a half necklace (eighths) |
| --- | --- | --- | --- |
|  |  |  |  |

## Extension

● Make some more necklaces by joining your links with those of a friend (or group of friends). How can you arrange/divide your links? How many times can you divide/arrange your links evenly?

| Whole necklace | Split evenly into three groups | Split again into three groups | Have you got enough to do it again? |
| --- | --- | --- | --- |
|  |  |  |  |

# Name patterns

## Activity introduction
● Using photocopiable page 59 and an interactive whiteboard, demonstrate to the children how to write out their names again and again, one letter in one box, in each of the grids (see below).

| H | O | L | L |
|---|---|---|---|
| Y | H | O | L |
| L | Y | H | O |
| L | L | Y | H |

● Provide each child with a copy of page 59. Encourage the children to complete all the grids on the sheet (they may not be able to write their name completely every time).
● Ask: *Which box does the first letter of your name show? Is it the same box in each grid? Why? Which grid does your name fit into perfectly? Why? Has anyone else got the same pattern as you? Why do you think that might be?*
● If children are struggling to see patterns clearly, they could make use of colour on their grids. Instruct them to colour the first letter of their name in one shade, the second letter in another, and so on. Ask: *What patterns can you see on the different grids?*

## Activity development
● Ask the children to look at the patterns of their name in each grid in relation to the size of grid. Ask if they can now predict what the pattern would be for other grids. For example, page 59 offers grids 2 × 2, 3 × 3, 4 × 4, 5 × 5 and 8 × 8. Can they predict the pattern in a 10 × 10 grid?
● Ask how they know what the answer might be. Can they show that they know (provide proof) their prediction is correct? Could they predict the pattern in bigger grids, such as a 20 × 20, 15 × 15, or 100 × 100?
● To support the extension of this line of enquiry, provide the children with a sheet of different empty grids (from 2 × 2 to 10 × 10).

## Review
● Gather examples of the name grids and identify to the group those children who have the same number of letters in their name.
● Compare and discuss what the children found out, recording on the whiteboard what they found interesting or surprising. Discuss the number patterns generated by the different-sized grids.
● Offer extension questions such as: *What if you use your surnames?*
● Discuss ideas and assess children's responses and their understanding of pattern relationships and structure in the number system.

### Next steps
● Use place names (your town, village or area) and draw from your current key vocabulary in other subjects (such as science or history).
● Encourage the children to form general statements about patterns and relationships. Ask them to test out their ideas on different examples.
● Make a class book of related name and number patterns for the book corner.

## Learning objectives
**(Y2) Use/apply strand:** Describe patterns and relationships involving numbers or shapes, make predictions and test these with examples.
**(Y2) Counting strand:** Read and write two-digit and three-digit numbers in figures and words; describe and extend number sequences and recognise odd and even numbers.
**(Y2) Knowledge strand:** Derive and recall multiplication facts for the 2, 5 and 10 times-tables and the related division facts; recognise multiples of 2, 5 and 10.
**(Y3) Use/apply strand:** Identify patterns and relationships involving numbers or shapes, and use these to solve problems.

## Expected prior knowledge
● Follow a line of enquiry, organise information and present and explain findings.
● Understand the relationship between different multiples and times-tables.

## You will need
Interactive whiteboard; photocopiable page 59 (one per child); coloured pens/pencils; sheet of empty square grids, from 2 × 2 to 10 × 10 (one per child).

## Key vocabulary
pattern, organise, properties, relationship, odd, even, sequence

## Brainteaser link
6: 'Crack the code' on page 13.

# Name patterns

◼ What pattern are you?

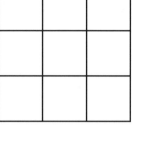

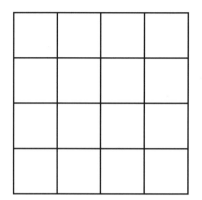

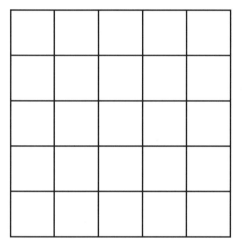

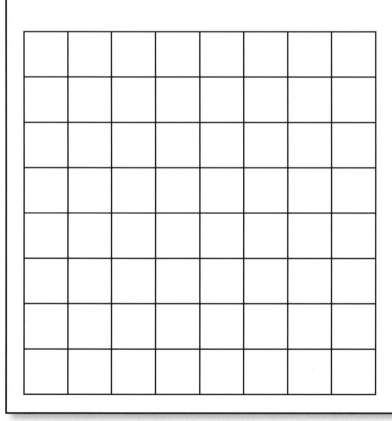

Illustration © Gaynor Berry

# Ten hens in pens

## Activity introduction

- Begin by looking at number bonds of 10 and the fact that addition can be done in any order: for example, 6 + 4 = 10 and 4 + 6 = 10.
- Look at 5 + 5 = 10 and then introduce 50 + 50 = 100. Discuss the relationship between the two additions and write down other examples (such as 3 + 3 = 6 and 30 + 30 = 60).
- Ask the children to write down some more family sentences like these on their whiteboards, giving them starting points. For example: *If you know 7 + 3 = 10, what else do you also know?* (70 + 30 = 100.)
- Using a 100-square, practise counting on in tens. Select a multiple of 10 and then together count up in tens to 100 from this number.

## Activity development

- Arrange the children into pairs and explain the following problem: *Farmer Fahed bought some new sheds for his hens. He asked carpenter Colin to make him some pens for the hens to sleep in at night. But carpenter Colin made different-sized sets of pens. The sheds hold 100 hens. The pens are in rows of 10 to help Farmer Fahed count his hens quickly at night. Arrange the rows of pens into groups of 100.*
- Provide each pair of children with a set of ten cards, prepared from photocopiable page 61. Note that the cards are proportional in size to the quantity they represent. Each shows a number of rows, with ten hens in pens in each row. Successful pairings will give ten rows of ten hens in pens. There is also one card that shows 100 hens in pens.
- The cards should be spread out face down. In turn, each child picks up a card, shows it to their partner and says how many hens they have (as a multiple of 10). They then calculate how many more hens they need to make a full shed of hens in pens (100). They must try to pick up the matching card to complement their first card (to total 100). If they are unsuccessful, they replace the card and wait until their next turn.
- When all five pairs are found, the children can play the game again and/or glue them onto paper, adding the appropriate number sentence next to each pairing (for example: 3 tens of hens + 7 tens of hens = 10 tens of hens). If this rhyming is confusing, just focus on the symbols.

## Review

- Offer a selection of ten hen number sentences (for example: 100 hens – 30 hens = 70 hens). Use these sentences to help the children make links between addition and subtraction.
- Offer a range of the addition and subtraction sentences and discuss the relationship with the units family (for example, 100 – 30 is related to 10 – 3).

### Learning objectives
**(Y1) Knowledge strand:** Count on or back in tens and use this knowledge to derive the multiples of 10 to the tenth multiple.
**(Y2) Knowledge strand:** Derive and recall all pairs of multiples of 10 with totals up to 100.
**(Y2) Knowledge strand:** Recognise multiples of 2, 5 and 10.
**(Y3) Knowledge strand:** Derive and recall sums and differences of multiples of 10 and number pairs that total 100.

### Expected prior knowledge
- Count to 100 in tens.
- Recall number bonds of 10.
- Order correctly multiples of 10 up to 100.

### You will need
Individual whiteboards; 100-square; cards from photocopiable page 61 (enlarge to A3 size, laminate and cut out the arrays of hens; one set of arrays per pair).

### Key vocabulary
multiples, complementary, addition, subtraction

### Brainteaser link
17: 'How many?' on page 16.

### Next steps
- Investigate (using the cards from photocopiable page 61) how to find three sets of hens that total 100 in the shed.
- The cards from page 61 can be altered to incorporate multiples of 5. Again, ask children to find pairs that total 100 (for example, 75 hens + 25 hens = 100).

Name ______________________________

# Ten hens in pens

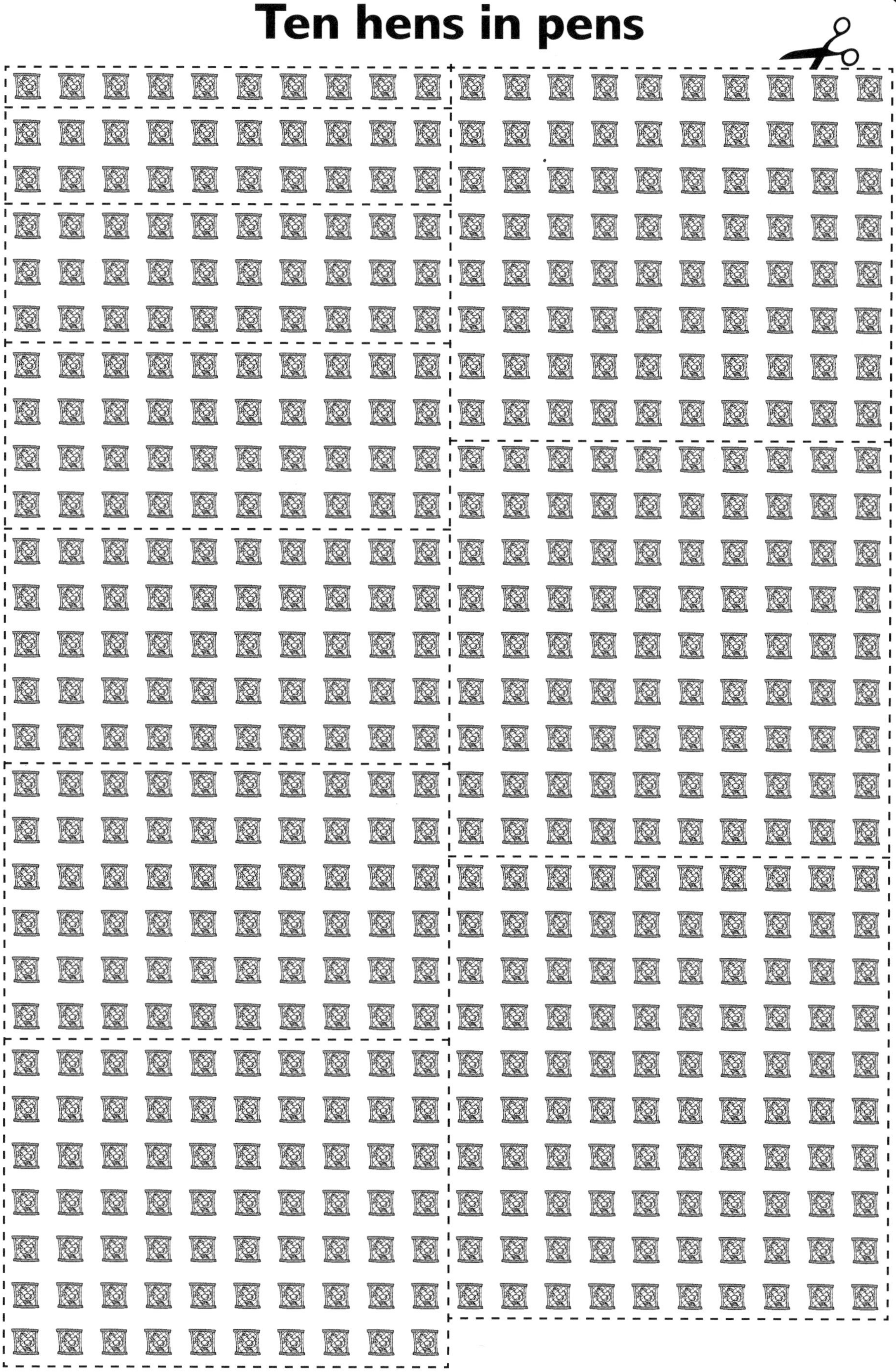

# Double trouble

## Activity introduction
- This activity is in two parts. The first part introduces/practises using doubles.
- Ask the children to draw the table below on individual whiteboards or paper, writing the numbers 1 to 10 in the first column.
- Now ask children to complete the table, doubling each number twice.

| Number | Double | Double |
|--------|--------|--------|
| 1 | 2 | 4 |
| 2 | 4 | 8 |
| 3 | 6 | 12 |
| 4... | 8 | 16 |

- If you think it appropriate, extend the task to include the numbers 11 and 12, to extend children's thinking beyond 10.
- Discuss any patterns the children recognise. Spend time on this activity as there are several patterns to explore and discuss.

## Activity development
- Provide each pair of children with photocopiable page 63. If you wish, demonstrate the game using an enlarged version of the page before the children start to play themselves. The instructions for the game are given on the page.
- Scores should be kept by writing in a book, on a whiteboard or using a calculator.

## Review
- Discuss the numbers scored most frequently and talk about any difficulties the children may have encountered.

## Learning objectives
**(Y1) Knowledge strand:** Count on or back in ones, twos, fives and tens and use this knowledge to derive the multiples of 2, 5 and 10 to the tenth multiple.
**(Y1) Knowledge strand:** Recall the doubles of all numbers to at least 10.
**(Y2) Knowledge strand:** Understand that halving is the inverse of doubling and derive and recall doubles of all numbers to 20, and the corresponding halves.
**(Y3) Knowledge strand:** Derive and recall all addition and subtraction facts for each number to 20, sums and differences of multiples of 10 and number pairs that total 100.

## Expected prior knowledge
- Understand and use multiples of 2, 5 and 10 to the tenth multiple.
- Recall the doubles of numbers from 1 to 10.
- Recall multiples of 10.

## You will need
Individual whiteboards or paper; photocopiable page 63 (one per pair); enlarged copy of photocopiable page 63 (optional); 1–6 dice (one per pair); calculators (optional).

## Key vocabulary
doubles, multiples, addition, multiplication

## Brainteaser link
3: 'Make 12' on page 12.

### Next steps
- As an extension to the introductory activity, ask the children to complete the table below. They should write down the multiples of 10 to 120, and double each number twice.

| Number | Double | Double |
|--------|--------|--------|
| 10 | 20 | 40 |
| 20 | 40 | 80 |
| 30 | 60 | 120 |
| 40... | 80 | 160 |

- Discuss any patterns the children discover and see whether they can spot the relationship with the first table (as, for example, double 3 is 6, so double 30 is 60).
- For an alternative game, use four dice (one with three black faces and three white faces, one with three faces marked + and three faces marked –, and two numbered 1–6). Depending on whether they throw a plus or a minus, children must mentally add or subtract the numbers on the two 1–6 dice and then double the answer (if the dice lands on the grey area of the board) or double it twice (if it lands on the white area).

# Double trouble

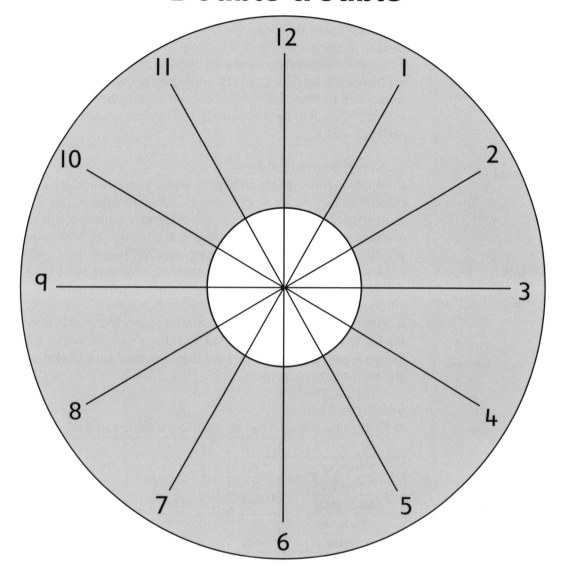

- Throw a dice onto the clockface board.
- Add the number on the dice to the number section the dice landed on.
- If it landed on the grey section, double the number. If it landed on the white section, double your number then double it again.

## Example

- If the dice lands showing a 5 on the number 7 grey section, work out 5 + 7 = 12 and then double to give 24.
- Keep a note of your scores. The winner is the player with the highest score after 12 throws.

# Postman Jim

**Learning objectives**
**(Y2) Use/apply strand:**
Solve problems involving addition [and] subtraction.
**(Y2) Calculate strand:** Add or subtract mentally a one-digit number... to or from any two-digit number.

**Expected prior knowledge**
● Add and subtract single- and two-digit numbers.

**You will need**
Photocopiable page 65 (one per child); paper and pencils.

**Key vocabulary**
difference, total, more, less

**Brainteaser link**
16: 'Birthday money' on page 16.

## Activity introduction
● Explain to the children that you are going to say a number and they need to respond with the number that is 2 more. For example: you say 32; children respond by saying 34. Repeat this several times.
● Change the activity to 2 less. For example: you say 28; children respond by saying 26. Again, repeat the activity several times.
● Establish that in each activity the difference between the numbers in each pair was 2.

## Activity development
● Introduce the problem on photocopiable page 65 and allow the children to investigate independently. They will need to use a trial and improvement method until a correct solution is achieved (see below).
● Ask questions to stimulate thinking and reasoning: *Which number will you start with? Is 20 a good starting number?* (Not if the number will be increased by 2 each time as the total will be far too large.)
● Remind the children that, in order for two adjacent numbers to have a difference of 2, they can either subtract 2 or add 2.
● When the first solution for Monday has been found, ask: *How close is the total on Tuesday?* Recognition that the totals are similar for these two days will help children realise they can start with similar numbers and then adjust them.

## Solution
● All of these answers can be reversed and the same total achieved.

|           | 1  | 2 | 3  | 4  | 5  | Total |
|-----------|----|---|----|----|----|-------|
| Monday    | 4  | 6 | 8  | 10 | 12 | 40    |
| Tuesday   | 6  | 8 | 10 | 8  | 10 | 42    |
| Wednesday | 5  | 7 | 5  | 7  | 9  | 33    |
| Thursday  | 4  | 6 | 4  | 2  | 4  | 20    |
| Friday    | 10 | 8 | 6  | 4  | 2  | 30    |

## Review
● Briefly share solutions. Ask the children to estimate and then calculate the total number of letters delivered over the five days.
● Encourage the use of jottings to support the calculation, and strategies such as adding numbers that total 10 or a multiple of 10 first. For example, in the solution for Monday, the 6 and 4 add to make 10 and the 12 and 8 add to make 20.
● Discuss strategies for the addition of the five two-digit numbers. The 40, 20 and 30 can be added together easily to total 90 as they are all multiples of 10. The 33 and 42 can be partitioned with the 30 and 40 totalling 70 and the 3 and 2 totalling 5, thus making 75.

> **Next steps**
> ● This activity requires a trial and improvement strategy. Don't be tempted to give too many clues if children are struggling. It may be preferable to tell them to leave the activity and return to it later.
> ● As an extension, ask: *Is it possible to achieve Monday's total of 40 with a difference of 3 between each house?* (Yes: 2, 5, 8, 11, 14).

# Postman Jim

Postman Jim delivers letters to each of the houses below. The number of letters delivered to each adjoining house has a difference of 2. These are the total number of letters delivered on each day:

| | |
|---|---|
| Monday | 40 letters in total |
| Tuesday | 42 letters in total |
| Wednesday | 33 letters in total |
| Thursday | 20 letters in total |
| Friday | 30 letters in total |

■ Work out the number of letters delivered to each house on each day.

*50 MATHS LESSONS · AGES 5-7*

Illustration © Gaynor Berry

# The toy shop

### Learning objectives
**(Y2) Use/apply strand:** Identify and record the information or calculation needed to solve a puzzle or problem; carry out the steps or calculations and check the solution in the context of the problem.
**(Y2) Calculate strand:** Use the symbols +, -, ×, ÷ and = to record and interpret number sentences involving all four operations; calculate the value of an unknown in a number sentence.

### Expected prior knowledge
● Calculate using money up to £2.

### You will need
5p and 10p coins; photocopiable page 67 (one per child).

### Key vocabulary
how many, weeks, save

### Brainteaser link
16: 'Birthday money' on page 16.

## Activity introduction
● Count as a group or class in steps of 10p and then 5p. Ask: *What does 10p add 5p total?* Establish the answer of 15p.
● Support the children in counting in steps of 15p by partitioning the 15p into 10p and 5p. Start with 10p and then add 5p and continue. Say the addition of 10p quietly and then the addition of 5p loudly to indicate that an addition of 15p has been completed. For example: 10p, (+5p), 15p, (+10p) 25p, (+5p) 30p, (+10p) 40p, (+5p) 45p... Hold up a 10p and 5p in turn to indicate which amount is being added.

## Activity development
● Introduce photocopiable page 67 and explain the problem. Ask: *How much money does Sam save each week?* Establish that the answer is 15p.
● Allow the children to work independently on the problem. Encourage them to make jottings to support their calculation of multiple groups of 15p. Remind them of the strategy they used to count in steps of 15p in the activity introduction.
● This activity involves multi-step operations. For example, finding the combined cost of the kite and the boat requires the initial subtraction of 50p - 35p = 15p. Then the addition of the two items 70p + 80p = £1.50 and finally 150 ÷ 15 = 10. As mentioned above, it should not be expected that children will record their steps in this formal manner; but this may be an opportunity, particularly for Year 2 children, to develop their use of formal number sentences.

## Solution
● Ball: 2 weeks; car: 4 weeks; kite and boat: 10 weeks (combined cost £1.50).

## Review
● Encourage the children to share their solutions and strategies with the rest of the class.
● Also consider how they have recorded their work. It is likely that they have recorded in informal and different ways. They can be introduced to horizontal number sentences to illustrate their calculations. For example, the calculation involving the toy car is 60 ÷ 15 = 4, or alternatively the problem can be represented by 4 × 15 = 60. For Year 1, the calculation can be represented as multiple addition (15p + 15p + 15p + 15p = 60p). It is important that children do not feel that their informal methods are incorrect but start to realise that there are alternative ways of recording their calculations.

### Next steps
● This activity uses the ability to count in equal steps to solve a problem. This links to the operation of multiplication.
● When counting in steps, draw children's attention to the connection between multiple addition and multiplication. Keep track of the count using fingers. For example 5, 10, 15, 20 results in four fingers held up. Ask: *How many 5s are there in 20?* The four fingers held up show that four 5s have been counted, resulting in 20.

Name _____

# The toy shop

Sam has 50p in pocket money each week. He spends 35p on sweets and saves the rest.

◀ How many weeks will it take him to save for the ball?

_____

_____

◀ How many weeks will it take him to save for the toy car?

_____

_____

◀ How many weeks will it take him to save for the kite and the boat?

_____

_____

Illustration © Gaynor Berry

# Difference in triangles

## Activity introduction

● On a whiteboard, draw a large version of the figure below:

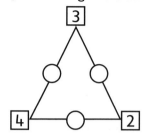

● Ask the children what they think they would have to do with this problem. Gather their ideas and discuss ways in which the missing numbers (that is, the differences between each pair of numbers) can be found.
● Discuss mental calculation and any strategies that the children find helpful.

## Activity development

● Provide each child with a copy of photocopiable page 69. Gather ideas about how they might approach the questions on the sheet. Suggest that they should try out their ideas on paper or a whiteboard first.
● Invite the children to work individually or in pairs through the examples on the photocopiable page. Point out that the order in which they find the difference between the pairs does not matter.
● Reinforce the associative nature of addition to check the children's answers, where the order of addition has no impact on the result.
● Encourage the children to collaborate in the challenge to identify the pattern (two of the difference numbers found add up to the other one). This will support less confident children and encourage ideas.

## Review

● Review the children's work. Show the pattern identified in the challenge on the figure already drawn on your whiteboard (see above).
● Ask the children if you could change the numbers in the square boxes without altering the differences between. You might want to start the idea off by altering the 2 to a 3 in the bottom right corner of the triangle and working through the difference idea. For example: *If this is now a 3 and there is a difference of 1, the number in the top square box must be ___? (4)*
● Can the children predict what other sets of numbers might be? Can they identify that the sets of numbers have to be consecutive (ordinal) numbers with 1, 1, 2 as the differences?

### Learning objectives
**(Y1) Use/apply strand:** Describe simple patterns and relationships involving numbers or shapes; decide whether examples satisfy given conditions.
**(Y1) Calculate strand:** Understand subtraction as 'take away' and find a 'difference' by counting up.
**(Y2) Use/apply strand:** Describe patterns and relationships involving numbers and shapes, make predictions and test these with examples.
**(Y2) Calculate strand:** Add or subtract mentally a one-digit number.

### Expected prior knowledge
● Able to subtract simple numbers mentally.
● Begin to be able to identify simple patterns in numbers.

### You will need
Photocopiable page 69 (one per child); pencils and paper.

### Key vocabulary
difference, take away, pattern, sequence, order, generalise

### Brainteaser link
4: 'Find the magic number' on page 12.

### Next steps
● If the children can identify the ordinal numbers in a 1, 1, 2 arrangement, can they generalise (in words) why they have to be consecutive?
● Ask the children to look at other sequences of differences (for example, 2, 2, 4) and offer examples of 8, 6 and 4 in the square boxes.
● Review the language specific to this activity (see 'Key vocabulary' left).

Name _____

# Difference in triangles

◼ Find the difference between the pairs of numbers in the figure below:

◼ Now try this:

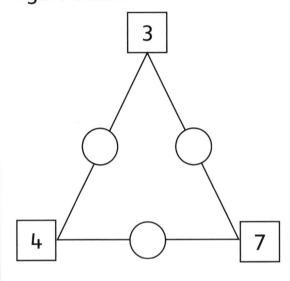
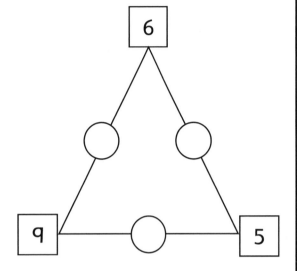

◼ What if the numbers in the boxes at each corner of the triangle were:

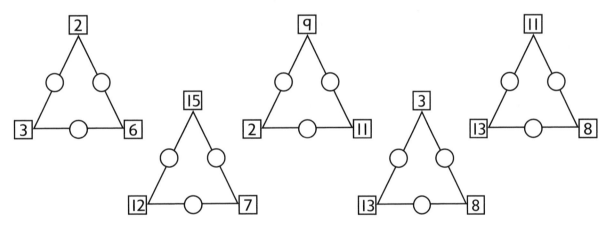

◼ Look at your answers. What do you notice about the 'differences between' numbers? Is there a pattern?

◼ Does this example fit into your pattern? Why/why not?

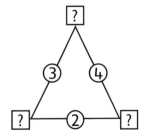

# Build a model

## Learning objectives
**(Y2) Use/apply strand:** Solve problems involving addition, subtraction, multiplication or division in contexts of numbers, measures or pounds and pence.
**(Y2) Calculate strand:** Add or subtract mentally a one-digit number or a multiple of 10 to or from any two-digit number; use practical and informal written methods to add and subtract two-digit numbers.

## Expected prior knowledge
● Add sums of money up to 20p and beyond.
● Calculate multiples of a number using multiplication or multiple addition.
● Sort and classify shapes according to their colour.

## You will need
Model made from a multi-coloured construction kit; photocopiable page 71 (one per child); multi-coloured construction pieces (each child needs enough pieces to build their own model); pencils and paper.

## Key vocabulary
cost, total

## Brainteaser links
2: 'The last penny' on page 11.
14: 'Football kit' on page 15.
16: 'Birthday money' on page 16.

## Activity introduction
● Present a model which has previously been made from a multi-coloured construction kit.
● Provide each child with photocopiable page 71. Draw their attention to the value of the different coloured pieces. Establish that the total cost of the model is calculated by adding the cost of each individual piece. Support the children in calculating the total cost of the model and demonstrate the use of jottings.
● Ask: *What would happen if I added two more blue pieces and a yellow piece to the model - what would the new cost be? What would happen if I took the blue piece away - what would the new cost be?*
● Ask the children to calculate the cost of the model on page 71.

## Activity development
● Give each child enough construction kit to build their own model. Ask them to calculate its cost, based on the values of the pieces listed on page 71 (if necessary, limit the size of the model to six pieces).
● Ask: *How much does your model cost? Does it cost more or less than your neighbour's model?*
● Ask each child to build a model with a value of 20p. Encourage them to use and discuss mental strategies for the addition. For example, the model on page 71 (which has a value of 20p) consists of:

| | |
|---|---|
| 2 yellow pieces at a cost of 1p each: | $2 \times 1p = 2p$ |
| 2 blue pieces at a cost of 5p each: | $2 \times 5p = 10p$ |
| 4 red pieces at a cost 2p each: | $4 \times 2p = 8p$ |
| Hence the total cost of the model is: | $2p + 10p + 8p = 20p$. |

## Solution
Models costing 20p can be made with the following combinations:

| Yellow 1p | Red 2p | Green 3p | Blue 5p | Other 10p | Total cost |
|---|---|---|---|---|---|
| 2 | 5 | 1 | 1 | | 20p |
| | 1 | 1 | 1 | 1 | 20p |
| 8 | 2 | 1 | 1 | | 20p |

There are of course other combinations. Encourage the children to reason that there will be many combinations and that a table can help them to record and check their findings.

## Review
● Share some of the models built by individuals or pairs of children with the group. Support the children in checking their value.
● Ask: *Is the biggest model always going to cost the most? Could you make a model which costs 20p by using only green pieces? Are there any other ways to make a model that costs 20p?*

### Next steps
● The activity can be extended by introducing a different total (for example, 50p or £1) instead of 20p.

Name _____

# Build a model

■ How much does this model cost to build?
Yellow pieces cost 1p
Red pieces cost 2p
Green pieces cost 3p
Blue pieces cost 5p
All other pieces cost 10p.

| Yellow | Yellow |
|--------|--------|
| Blue | Blue |

| Red | Red | Red | Red |
|-----|-----|-----|-----|

■ Build a model of your own and calculate its value.
■ Can you build a model with a value of 20p?

# Fraction pairs

## Learning objectives
**(Y2) Use/apply strand:** Solve problems involving addition, subtraction, multiplication or division in contexts of numbers.
**(Y3) Calculate strand:** Find unit fractions of numbers and quantities (for example, $1/2$, $1/3$, $1/4$ and $1/6$ of 12 litres).

## Expected prior knowledge
● Recognise and work out halves and quarters.

## You will need
Individual whiteboards; photocopiable page 73 (one per child); scissors (one pair per child).

## Key vocabulary
half, quarter

## Brainteaser links
4: 'Find the magic number' on page 12.
7: 'What's my rule?' on page 13.

## Activity introduction
● Revise unit fractions. Show four objects and ask the children to illustrate on their whiteboards ½ of 4.
● Ask: *What does the term 'one half' mean?* Establish that to divide something in half means to split it into two equal parts.
● Ask: *Show me ¼ of 4.* Establish that to divide something into quarters means to split it into four equal parts.

## Activity development
● Introduce photocopiable page 73 and ask the children to pair the cards that have the same answer. Ideally, they should cut out the cards so that they can be moved around and matched.
● Encourage the children to look for patterns (for example, ½ of 4 is the same as ¼ of 8). Ask: *What do you notice about these two number sentences? Can you explain why they are the same?*
● Children who find these questions challenging may find it helpful to use objects to demonstrate that both number sentences give the same total.
● Encourage the children to look for patterns and relationships. This is fundamental to developing understanding in mathematics. In each pair, one whole number is double that of the other; the number on the bottom (the denominator) of the fraction is also doubled. The idea of equivalence is also important (for example, ½ of 4 = ¼ of 8).

## Solution

| $1/2$ of 4 | $1/4$ of 8 |
|---|---|
| $1/2$ of 6 | $1/4$ of 12 |
| $1/2$ of 8 | $1/4$ of 16 |
| $1/2$ of 10 | $1/4$ of 20 |
| $1/3$ of 6 | $1/6$ of 12 |
| $1/3$ of 9 | $1/6$ of 18 |
| $1/3$ of 3 | $1/6$ of 6 |
| $1/5$ of 10 | $1/10$ of 20 |

## Review
● Share solutions and discuss any patterns.
● Write the number 12 on the board, and ask the children to find as many fractions of it as possible. Ask for $1/2$ of 12, $1/3$ of 12, $1/4$ of 12, $1/6$ of 12 and $1/12$ of 12.
● Ask: *Is it possible to find $1/5$ of 12?* Explore with concrete materials, dividing 12 into 5 equal parts. Establish that it is not possible to do so.
● Begin to support children in making the link between fractions and division. The attempt to divide 12 into five equal parts demonstrates that 12 cannot be divided by 5 without a remainder.

## Next steps
● The main activity explores fractions as part of a quantity. Children will probably have also explored fractions as part of a shape. Help them to make the link between these two types of activity. Emphasise that a fraction is an equal part, whether this is of a shape or a quantity.

# Fraction pairs

■ Pair the cards which are the same.

| | | | |
|---|---|---|---|
| $\frac{1}{2}$ of 4 | $\frac{1}{5}$ of 10 | $\frac{1}{4}$ of 20 | $\frac{1}{2}$ of 8 |
| $\frac{1}{3}$ of 9 | $\frac{1}{10}$ of 20 | $\frac{1}{6}$ of 18 | $\frac{1}{4}$ of 12 |
| $\frac{1}{6}$ of 6 | $\frac{1}{4}$ of 8 | $\frac{1}{2}$ of 6 | $\frac{1}{3}$ of 6 |
| $\frac{1}{6}$ of 12 | $\frac{1}{2}$ of 10 | $\frac{1}{4}$ of 16 | $\frac{1}{3}$ of 3 |

# Arrays

## Activity introduction

- Ask the children to take a handful of linking cubes and put them together into a rectangular shape (technically this is a cuboid, but for this activity the focus is on rectangles).
- Ask: *How many squares are there on the top face of your shape? How many rows are there? How many columns are there?*
- Select one of the rectangles and explore it together: for example, 12 cubes arranged in 3 rows of 4. Ask: *How many squares can you see in each row?* (4) *How many rows can you see?* (3) *How many squares are there altogether?* (12)
- Establish that the rows of 4 can be seen as groups of 4. Three groups of 4 is equal to 12. This can be written as a number sentence: 3 × 4 = 12.
- Now explore how many squares are in each column. (3) In the same manner as above, establish that four groups of 3 is also equal to 12.
- Ask: *Could we put the 12 in rows of 5 and still make a rectangle?* Try this out and demonstrate that it will not work.

## Activity development

- Provide each child with photocopiable page 75. Explain the meaning of 'array' in this context (that it is a quantity – a number of squares – arranged into a rectangle).
- There is more than one array for each of the numbers; let the children discover this for themselves. Prompt their thinking by asking: *Are there any other ways that you could make a rectangle with 12 squares?*
- Arrays are a powerful image for developing understanding of multiplication. They demonstrate the fact that multiplication is commutative – for example, that 3 × 4 is the same as 4 × 3.

## Solution

| | |
|---|---|
| 4 | 1 × 4, 2 × 2 |
| 6 | 1 × 6, 2 × 3 |
| 8 | 1 × 8, 2 × 4 |
| 12 | 1 × 12, 2 × 6, 3 × 4 |
| 18 | 1 × 18, 2 × 9, 3 × 6 |

## Review

- Discuss the solutions and highlight alternative solutions.
- Draw the children's attention to the arrays that demonstrate the fact that multiplication is commutative, such as 3 × 4 and 4 × 3. These are in fact the same arrays, presented in different orientations.

### Next steps

- Challenge the children to make arrays with larger numbers. Ask: *How many different arrays can you make with the number 24?* (Four: 1 × 24, 2 × 12, 3 × 8, 4 × 6.)

---

### Learning objectives
**(Y2) Use/apply strand:** Solve problems involving addition, subtraction, multiplication or division in contexts of numbers.
**(Y2) Calculate strand:** Represent repeated addition and arrays as multiplication.

### Expected prior knowledge
- Understand multiplication as repeated addition.

### You will need
Linking cubes (a handful per child); photocopiable page 75 (one per child); colouring pens/pencils.

### Key vocabulary
array, row, column

### Brainteaser links
4: 'Find the magic number' on page 12.
10: 'The answer is...' on page 14.

# Arrays

■ Colour in the correct number of squares to make rectangles with the following number of squares:
4, 6, 8, 12, 18 (4 and 6 have already been done for you).

# Make a sentence

## Activity introduction
● The activity could be introduced by using a simplified version of the game. Use a set of numbers displayed on an interactive whiteboard or stuck on a whiteboard so that all the children can see. Display the symbol cards +, – and =. Explain to the children that you are going to make a number sentence using two number cards and two symbol cards (for example, 4 + ? = 9) and display these on the board. Tell them that you are going to say the whole sentence (including the missing digit: for example, four plus five equals nine) and they have to check whether you are correct.
● Ask the children to discuss with a partner whether they can devise a number sentence using only two number cards and two symbol cards. Gather their ideas and discuss what the potential difficulties are, and the different approaches to thinking up a number sentence.

## Activity development
● Provide each pair of children with a set of cards prepared using photocopiable page 77. Give them time to devise their sentences.
● There are several options for this activity: the children can play in pairs or in groups of up to four players; they can play individually or pair against pair (which can offer support for those who might want it).
● Each player or 'team' has ten turns to create a number sentence.
● The children should write down their scores. They can also write down their number sentences as evidence, as well as collecting the number cards they have used in a number sentence.

## Review
● Discuss any patterns the children discovered that will help them become more efficient in thinking about and finding new number sentences.
● Discuss the most 'friendly' numbers used, and talk about any difficulties the children may have encountered.
● If no one, or not many, went on to use the × or ÷ symbols, ask the group to come up with sentences using these symbols. Discuss any difficulties and identify the prior knowledge and understanding they need to be able to complete these sentences.

### Next steps
● This game can be extended for those children confident in their tables by asking them to concentrate on the × and ÷ symbols. Many will be able to create a sentence with '× 2' or '× 5' in it.
● Review the vocabulary specific to the activity (see 'Key vocabulary' left).

---

### Learning objectives
**(Y1) Use/apply strand:** Answer a question by selecting and sorting information.
**(Y2) Use/apply strand:** Identify and record the information or calculation needed to solve a puzzle or problem; carry out the steps or calculations and check the solution in the context of the problem.
**(Y2) Calculate strand:** Use the symbols +, -, ×, ÷ and = to record and interpret number sentences involving all four operations; calculate the value of an unknown in a number sentence.
**(Y3) Calculate strand:** Add or subtract mentally combinations of one-digit and two-digit numbers.

### Expected prior knowledge
● Add and subtract mentally.
● Understand and use the four operations.
● Begin to calculate the value of an unknown in a number sentence.

### You will need
Interactive whiteboard (or ordinary whiteboard); prepared set of cards from photocopiable page 77 (one per child/pair/small group of up to four); paper and pencils; calculators (optional).

### Key vocabulary
sentence, add, minus, subtract, equals, times, divided

### Brainteaser link
16: 'Birthday money' on page 16.

# Make a sentence

| | | | | |
|---|---|---|---|---|
| 1 | 2 | 3 | 4 | 5 |
| 6 | 7 | 8 | 9 | 10 |
| 11 | 12 | 13 | 14 | 15 |
| 16 | 17 | 18 | 19 | 20 |
| 21 | 22 | 23 | 24 | 25 |
| 26 | 27 | 28 | 29 | 30 |
| + | − | × | ÷ | = |

# More or less

## Activity introduction

● To introduce this activity, an interactive whiteboard with dice software could be used. You could start by playing against the children (for example, see who gets the best of three throws each). Model the process for playing the game, following the instructions on photocopiable page 79.

● Next, hand out copies of page 79 to pairs of children. Tell them to follow the instructions on the sheet if they cannot remember them.

● When the children have thrown the dice ten times each, pairs can play against other pairs before comparing their results and discussing the most useful and the least useful dice scores.

## Activity development

● When the children have completed photocopiable page 79, the basic idea can be developed in different ways.

● For example, instead of adding the scores on the two 1-6 dice, the children could create a new number by designating one of the scores a 'tens' number and the other a 'ones' number. So if they throw 3, 5 and -10, they would choose 3 to be the 'tens' number and 5 to be the 'ones' number, making 35 (because the aim is to score as low as possible), and then take away 10, leaving a total of 25.

● Let the children play a similar game to the one outlined on page 79, but this time provide them with two 1-6 dice and one showing +1, +1, -1, -1, +10, -10.

● Alternatively, use three 1-6 dice and one showing +1, -1, +10, -10, +100, -100. Instead of adding the numbers together, the children should designate one of the scores a 'hundreds' number, one a 'tens' number and the third a 'ones' number. So if they throw 1, 2, 6 and +1, they would choose 1 to be the 'hundreds' number, 2 to be the 'tens' number and 6 to be the 'ones' number, making 126, and then add the 1 to get a total of 127. Again, the smallest total wins.

## Review

● At the end of the session, gather the children's ideas about which were the most helpful and least helpful dice scores. Ask them to articulate why they think this.

● Ask them what other game(s) they could play using dice to generate numbers. Gather the rules for these new games and ask the children why rules are important for games.

### Learning objectives
**(Y1) Counting strand:** Say the number that is 1 more or 1 less than any given number, and 10 more or less for multiples of 10.
**(Y2) Calculate strand:** Add or subtract mentally a one-digit number or a multiple of 10 to or from any two-digit number; use practical and informal written methods to add and subtract two-digit numbers.
**(Y3) Use/apply strand:** Follow a line of enquiry by deciding what information is important; make and use lists, tables and graphs to organise and interpret the information.

### Expected prior knowledge
● Understand the concept of 1 more/less and 10 more/less.
● Add on or take away 1 and add on 10 mentally.

### You will need
Interactive whiteboard with dice software (optional); photocopiable page 79 (one per pair); dice (two numbered 1-6 and one showing +1, +1, -1, -1, +10, +10 per pair); extra dice (optional).

### Key vocabulary
place value, tens, units, ones, more, less, least, total

### Brainteaser link
8: 'Is it true? (1)' on page 13.

### Next steps
● There are many variations on this activity (for example, the child with the highest number wins rather than the lowest, or different numbered dice could be used). If you were looking at adding/taking away 5 for example, these two functions could be ascribed to another 'more/less' dice.
● Review the vocabulary specific to the activity (see 'Key vocabulary' left).

Name _____

# More or less

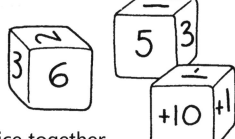

Two dice show the numbers 1–6. The other shows +1, +1, –1, –1, +10 and +10.

■ Play this game with a partner.

■ Take turns in throwing all three dice together.

■ Each time you throw:

■ Add up the two numbers, then add/take away 1, or add 10, as the third dice instructs you. For example, if you throw 5, 6 and –1, add 5 and 6 to get 11, then take away 1 to get 10.

■ Write down your score below.

■ After ten turns each, who has the highest/lowest score? The lowest score wins.

■ Which was the most useful/least useful dice score of all? Why?

| Player 1 | Player 2 |
|---|---|
|  |  |
|  |  |
|  |  |
|  |  |
|  |  |
|  |  |
|  |  |
|  |  |
|  |  |
|  |  |
| **Total:** | **Total:** |

Illustration © Gaynor Berry

# Subtraction sacks

## Learning objectives
**(Y1) Calculate strand:** Understand subtraction as 'take away' and find a 'difference' by counting up.
**(Y1) Calculate strand:** Use the vocabulary related to addition and subtraction and symbols to describe and record addition and subtraction number sentences.
**(Y2) Calculate strand:** Understand that subtraction is the inverse of addition and vice versa; use this to derive and record related addition and subtraction number sentences.
**(Y2) Use/apply strand:** Present solutions to puzzles and problems in an organised way.

## Expected prior knowledge
● Subtract simple numbers mentally.
● Identify simple patterns in numbers.

## You will need
Two sacks/bags with three big two-digit numbers in one and two small one- and two-digit numbers in the other; number lines/squares (optional); photocopiable page 81 (one per child/pair); pencils and paper; playing cards (optional).

## Key vocabulary
subtract, difference, take away, sentence, big, bigger, small, smaller, calculation

## Activity introduction
● Using your two prepared sacks/bags, ask one of the children to pull out one of the numbers from each bag. Discuss which number is the smaller and which is the bigger.
● Ask the children what they would write down if you asked them to subtract the smaller number from the bigger number.
● Write the sentence on the board and discuss what information the sentence tells us.
● Discuss the strategies the children use and resources that might support their thinking, such as number lines.
● Repeat the process. Take out the remaining number from the big sack and ask the children how many subtraction sentences they could make altogether, using all the numbers (find all possibilities).
● Discuss with the children how you might set out your sentences so that you can check you have all possibilities.

## Activity development
● Provide each child or pair of children with photocopiable page 81. Explain that there are more numbers in these sacks. Read through the questions with the group to ensure clarity and understanding, and offer the challenge of finding all the possible subtraction sentences.
● If the children are able to complete this activity, ask them to work on the extension question on the photocopiable page, which is exploratory.

## Review
● Review the children's ideas and completed sentences (they should have found 35 sentences).
● Discuss the extension question and any difficulties or problems the children might have had. Emphasise that subtraction is the inverse of addition and vice versa.
● Can the children predict how many subtraction sentences they could make with the different numbers in the two sacks? Why? (7 numbers × 5 numbers = 35 sentences.)

### Next steps
● Using a pack of playing cards, take two cards from the pack to make up a two-digit number (for example, 8 and 3 could be used to make 83 or 38). Now subtract your smaller number from your bigger number. Identify the pattern: digit sum will add up to 9. For example, 83 - 38 = 45 (4 + 5 = 9).
● Review the vocabulary specific to the activity (see 'Key vocabulary' left).

# Subtraction sacks

The numbers in the 'big' sack are 'bigger' than the numbers in the 'small' sack.

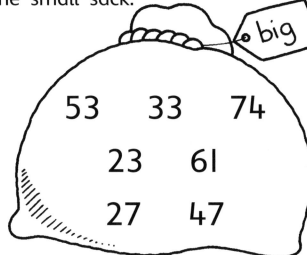

- ◢ Choose one number from each sack.
- ◢ Subtract the small number from the big number.
- ◢ How many different subtraction sentences can you make in this way?

_____

_____

_____

_____

**Extension**
- ◢ Now add the small number to the big number.
- ◢ Subtract your small answer from your large answer.
- ◢ What do you notice?
- ◢ Try again and see if you were right.

_____

_____

Illustration © Gaynor Berry

# Investigating triangles

**Learning objectives**
**(Y2) Use/apply strand:**
Describe patterns and relationships involving numbers or shapes, make predictions and test these with examples.
**(Y2) Shape strand:**
Visualise common 2D shapes; sort, make and describe shapes, referring to their properties.

**Expected prior knowledge**
● Understand that a 2D shape is a space enclosed by lines.

**You will need**
Sets of equilateral triangles (one per child) (these can be cut from the photocopiable page but card or plastic ones would be preferable); photocopiable page 83 (one per child); scissors; glue.

**Key vocabulary**
2D shape, side, triangle

**Brainteaser links**
9: 'Is it true? (2)' on page 14.
19: 'Rough snack symmetry' on page 17.

## Activity introduction
● Ask a child to take some of the equilateral triangles and put them together to create a 2D shape. With the class, discuss the shape in terms of its properties.
● Ask: *How many triangles have been used? How many sides does it have? How many corners/vertices does it have? Are all its sides the same length?*

## Activity development
● Hand out copies of photocopiable page 83 to each child. Explain that the challenge is to make shapes with differing numbers of sides using the equilateral triangles. The children may work independently or in pairs.
● If the children are going to use paper triangles from the sheet, supply them with scissors to cut them out. These may be glued down on a separate piece of paper once a solution has been found for each challenge.
● All shape activities should be used as an opportunity to explore the properties of shape and develop use of the associated language. It may be possible to extend the language of more able children beyond age expectations. This will support them in explaining their ideas. It is important that when new vocabulary is introduced, the children have the opportunity to discuss and explore its meaning.

## Solutions

A 4-sided shape, using 2 triangles

A 4-sided shape, using 3 triangles

A 6-sided shape, using 4 triangles

A 7-sided shape, using 5 triangles

A 15-sided shape, using 5 triangles

## Review
● Share the children's solutions. Ask: *Are the shapes all the same?* Some that appear different may be the same but presented in different orientations.

### Next steps
● The first four solutions involve tessellation of the equilateral triangles. A tessellation is an arrangement of shapes that fit together to create another shape with no gaps or overlaps.
● Explore shapes that tessellate and those that do not.

Name _____

# Investigating triangles

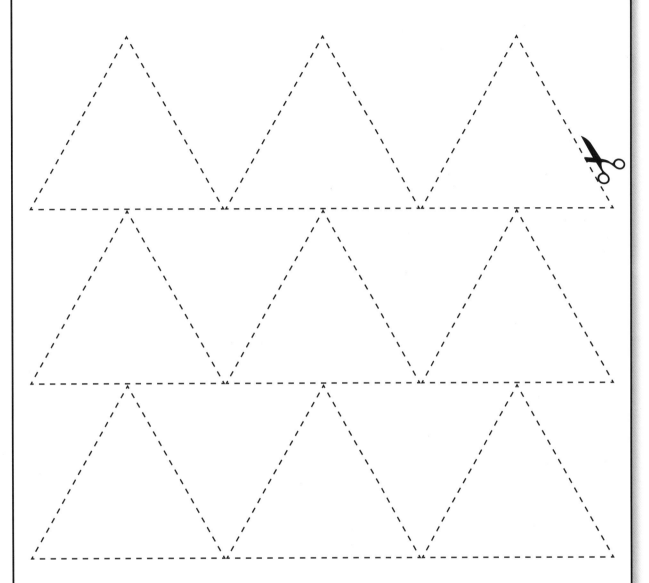

■ Cut out the triangles above.

■ What other shapes can you make by joining the triangles together?

■ Can you make a 4-sided shape using 2 triangles?

■ Can you make a 4-sided shape using 3 triangles?

■ Can you make a 6-sided shape using 4 triangles?

■ Can you make a 7-sided shape using 5 triangles?

■ Make a shape with the greatest possible number of sides.

# Walk to school

## Learning objectives
**(Y1) Use/apply strand:**
Describe a puzzle or problem using numbers, practical materials and diagrams; use these to solve the problem and set the solution in the original context.
**(Y2) Shape strand:** Follow and give instructions involving position, direction and movement.

## Expected prior knowledge
● Use and apply the language of movement.

## You will need
Photocopiable page 85; floor obstacles; squared paper (for each child/pair).

## Key vocabulary
left, right, north, south, east, west

## Activity introduction
● Introduce or remind the children of the directional language of north, south, east and west. Ask them to stand up. Tell them they are facing north.
● Put a sign up on the wall to remind them which direction north is.
● Now ask them to move two steps towards north. Then ask them to turn and move two steps towards east. Continue with this activity until all the children are confident in their use of north, south, east and west.
● Ask the children to work in pairs, giving each other instructions as above.

## Activity development
● Introduce photocopiable page 85. Explain to the children that the task is to record Sam's possible routes to school, using the language of north, south, east and west.
● The children use the smaller grids to record their solutions and write the instructions underneath, using the appropriate language.
● Encourage them to check whether they have found all of the solutions. If they find this difficult, support them by asking questions: *Have you found all the routes that cross the middle of the grid? Have you found all the routes that go north first?*

## Solutions
N, E, N, E (as shown)
N, N, E, E
N, N, E, S, E, N
E, N, N, E
E, N, E, N
E, E, N, N

## Review
● Represent Sam's journey using obstacles on the floor. Ask the children to demonstrate their solutions by instructing another child to walk the route.
● Record the routes on the board. Have they all been found? Ask: *Will the possible routes from school to home be the same as those from home to school?*

## Next steps
● Ask a child to draw, on squared paper, a home and school in a different position from the grid on photocopiable page 85. They then explore and record the number of possible routes from home to school.
● The above activities involve the use of spatial skills. Some children may be able in their use of number, but may find spatial problems more difficult. The practical exploration of spatial problems will help to develop these skills. Some may need practical help to distinguish left and right turns. A sticker placed on their right hand may help in the early stages.

# Walk to school

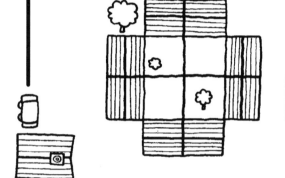
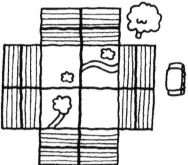
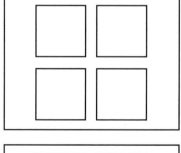

**School**

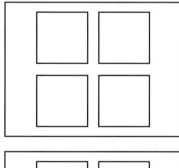
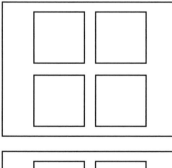

**Home**

Sam likes to take different routes on his walk to school.

◾ How many different routes can he take?

◾ Describe the routes using the language of north, south, east and west.

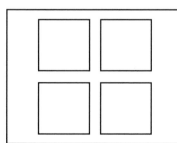
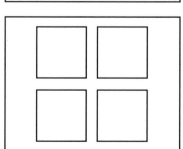
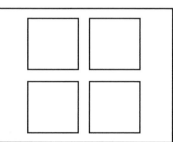

Illustration © Gaynor Berry

# Making shapes from squares

## Learning objectives
**(Y2) Use/apply strand:** Describe patterns and relationships involving numbers or shapes, make predictions and test these with examples.
**(Y2) Shape strand:** Follow and give instructions involving position, direction and movement.
**(Y3) Use/apply strand:** Identify patterns and relationships involving numbers or shapes, and use these to solve problems.
**(Y3) Use/apply strand:** Follow a line of enquiry by deciding what information is important; make and use lists, tables and graphs to organise and interpret the information.
**(Y3) Use/apply strand:** Describe and explain methods, choices and solutions to puzzles and problems, orally and in writing, using pictures and diagrams.

## Expected prior knowledge
● Use mental and written methods efficiently to add several two-digit numbers.

## You will need
Squares made from card (at least three); enlarged version of photocopiable page 87 (optional); photocopiable page 87 (one per pair/group).

## Key vocabulary
shape, side, match, equal length, point edge, pattern

## Brainteaser links
6: 'Crack the code' on page 13.
8: 'Is it true? (1)' on page 13.

## Activity introduction
● Show the children three card squares. Offer a general statement to the group (for example: *There are only two ways of putting these three squares together to make a different shape*). Show them a row (or tower) of three squares and a shape with two squares side by side with one underneath (as on photocopiable page 87). Discuss the fact that although each shape produced can be moved around (rotated) and might look like a different shape, it is still the same shape. Ask: *Can you make any other shapes with three squares? How will you know you have found all the possible shapes? How will you present your findings to the class?*
● Introduce a method of recording the shapes, perhaps making all possibilities using card squares first, then placing them on the grid on an enlarged copy of photocopiable page 87.
● Progress to drawing the shapes as a record of all the shapes made. Ask related questions: *If you move this shape around a right angle* (demonstrate rotating the shape through 90°), *is it still the same shape?*

## Activity development
● Provide each pair or group with photocopiable page 87. Explain to the children that they will be investigating the range of shapes they can make with four squares. Ask them to cut out the four squares on the page and use these to investigate the possible shapes.
● Again, encourage the children to record the shapes they make by placing them on the grid on page 87, and then drawing them.
● Develop the children's ideas and thoughts about how to record their findings so that there is a variety that can be discussed in the review session. Continue to encourage the way in which the children develop a systematic and structured approach to their exploration.

## Review
● Begin this section by gathering selected children's recordings of the shapes found. After the children have presented their work, discuss which method of recording was the clearest.
● Ask the children what was difficult and challenging.

### Next steps
● To extend this activity, explore a different shape that tessellates: for example, use three equilateral triangle cards. Ask the children to predict how many shapes they think they could make with these. Ask: *Is it the same number of shapes as with the squares? How could I record my findings?*

# Making shapes from squares

■ Using three squares, are there just two unique shapes you can make?

■ How many shapes can you make with four squares?

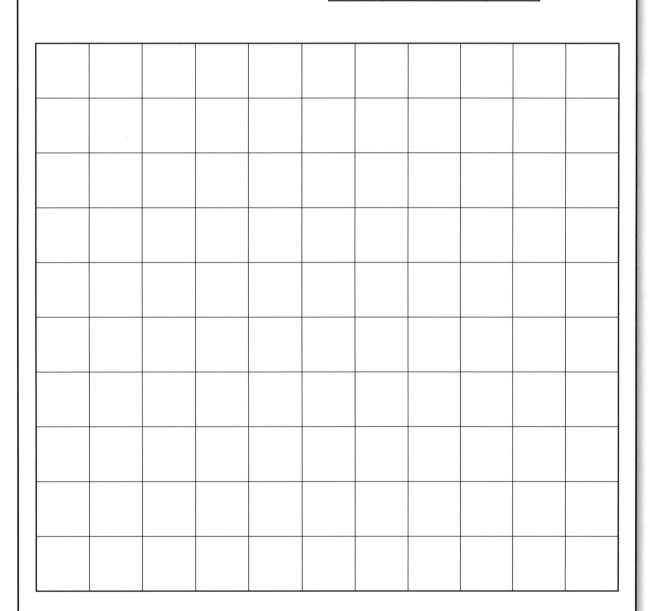

# Trying triangles

## Activity introduction
● This activity explores the properties of equilateral triangles and their relationship with each other. It will also extend those children who are beginning to explore mathematical structure and develop their mathematical thinking.
● Draw a large triangle with two upward pointing triangles along the base, as below.

● Ask: *How many triangles can you see?* Draw around the top triangle with a different coloured pen/chalk, cover with one you made earlier, or with pre-drawn triangles if you are using an interactive whiteboard. Ask: *How many more triangles can you see?*
● Now draw the triangle presented on photocopiable page 89, with three upward pointing triangles at the base.
● Ask the same questions as before. Encourage further investigation by asking: *If we add up all the upward pointing triangles together with all the downward pointing triangles, we have 6 + 3 = 9 triangles. Is this how many triangles you found? Can you see any bigger triangles inside?* (Answer: 3 more, plus the whole shape, making 13 altogether.)
● Ask: *If you had another row along the bottom of your triangle, how many triangles will you be able to find?* Discuss and then explore the question.

## Activity development
● Using the set of triangles showing three pointing upwards on the base of the diagram, explore the numbers of upward pointing triangles and downward pointing triangles.
● Ask the children if they can predict how many triangles would be in a set where there were six upward pointing triangles on the base of the set. Ask: *How many upward pointing triangles? How many downward pointing triangles?*
● Ask the children to identify any patterns they see between upward/downward pointing triangles and the total number of triangles.

## Review
● Review the children's findings and any patterns identified. Can they generalise (in words) any patterns they have found? Discuss their findings, identifying any structure or pattern the children discovered.

### Next steps
● Investigate rows of triangles using numbers in the rows (see below). Can the children identify a pattern growth? Can they predict what the fifth row would be? What the tenth row would be? The hundredth row?

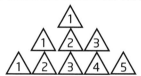

# Trying triangles

# Square crazy

## Activity introduction

● Using 'dotty squares' on an interactive whiteboard or with an overhead projector, ask the children if they could draw a square using the dots. Ask if they can explain why it is a square. Demonstrate how to draw three or four squares using different lengths on the horizontal line and measure the side lengths by counting the dots (1 dot, 2 dots and so on).

● Ask the children to identify squares that are the same and squares that are different in size (a ruler could be used here). Ensure that the children are aware of the area (in terms of number of small squares) of each of the squares identified.

## Activity development

● Provide each child with photocopiable page 91. Explain that there are 13 squares 'hidden' amongst the dots and their task is to find as many as they can. Check that they can explain clearly how they know they have drawn a square.

● Encourage the children to collaborate in their investigations and compare their findings with each other's.

● Children could be challenged to investigate how many squares a 4 × 4 dotty square would contain. Supply dotty paper for this activity.

● Ask questions such as: *How many squares can you find within the 4 × 4 square? How many different-sized squares are there?*

## Review

● Gather the children's answers for each sized grid. Discuss the differences and talk about any difficulties the children may have had locating squares.

● Draw a rectangle on dotty squared paper and ask children how they would describe the size of the rectangle.

● Discuss the differences between counting up the side lengths and counting the squares inside the shape.

### Next steps
● Explore rectangles further, counting how many rectangles can be drawn within a specific set of dots.
● Explore how many squares the children can count within each rectangle drawn.
● Explore the differences between the number of inside squares and the lengths of the sides for the rectangles drawn. This will help the children develop a deeper understanding and knowledge of perimeter and area.

## Learning objectives
**(Y1) Measure strand:** Estimate, measure, weigh and compare objects, choosing and using suitable uniform non-standard or standard units and measuring instruments.
**(Y2) Use/apply strand:** Describe patterns and relationships involving numbers or shapes, make predictions and test these with examples.
**(Y2) Measure strand:** Estimate, compare and measure lengths, weights and capacities, choosing and using standard units.
**(Y4) Measure strand:** Draw rectangles and measure and calculate their perimeters; find the area of rectilinear shapes drawn on a square grid by counting squares.

## Expected prior knowledge
● Recognise a square as a shape with four straight sides of the same length.
● Understand a half and/or quarter turn.

## You will need
Interactive whiteboard or overhead projector; photocopiable page 91 (one per child); rulers and pencils; dotty squared paper (enough for each child to explore the side length and area of squares).

## Key vocabulary
square, rectangle, length, sides, inside area, outside length (perimeter)

## Brainteaser links
13: 'Shoe size' on page 15.
15: 'Clothes size' on page 16.

# Square crazy

Here are 13 dots.
- Can you see a 3 dot × 3 dot square?
- Can you see a 2 dot × 2 dot square? How many can you see?

The 13 dots are turned half a right angle on the page.
- Can you see any more squares?
- Can you see any squares within squares?

# Dinner ladies

## Learning objectives

**(Y1) Use/apply strand:** Describe simple patterns and relationships involving numbers or shapes; decide whether examples satisfy given conditions.
**(Y2) Use/apply strand:** Describe patterns and relationships involving numbers or shapes, make predictions and test these with examples.
**(Y3) Shape strand:** Read and record the vocabulary of position, direction and movement.

## Expected prior knowledge

- Work in a group.
- Use logical thinking to sort information.
- Recognise similarities and differences in patterns and problems.

## You will need

Interactive whiteboard (optional); photocopiable page 93 (one per pair/child); paper (preferably squared).

## Key vocabulary

grid, efficient, systematic approach, reason, justify

## Brainteaser link

6: 'Crack the code' on page 13.

## Activity introduction

- On an interactive whiteboard, draw a square to represent a school playground. Explain to the children that when they are in the playground at lunchtime, an adult has to be on duty to look after them.
- Now draw a smaller square inside the first one, to represent a mobile classroom (see diagram on page 93). Ask the children where a dinner lady would have to stand in order to be able see all the children if a mobile classroom was placed in the middle of the playground.
- Ask further questions to guide children's thinking: *Would the dinner lady have to move? Why?*
- Allow the children thinking time and gather their ideas of how the dinner lady would have to move. Establish that there are two significant viewpoints (at the diagonal), as shown on the photocopiable page.
- Discuss the children's justifications for their ideas. Raise the point that the more dinner ladies a school employs, the more expensive it is.
- Finally, discuss the fact that, for the playground in the illustration to be safe, two dinner ladies are needed to watch the children.

## Activity development

- Provide each child (or pair) with photocopiable page 93. Ask them to look at the diagram showing two mobile classrooms. As before, allow thinking time before gathering their ideas and justifications. Ask them to add the position of the dinner ladies needed in a playground with two mobile classrooms to the diagram.
- There are five different-shaped playgrounds with different numbers of mobile classrooms in each. Ask the children to find the minimum number of dinner ladies needed for each playground.
- The final task involves investigating further different-shaped playgrounds and numbers of mobile classrooms. Ask the children if they can spot any patterns emerging between the shape of the playground and the numbers of mobile classrooms.
- This activity provides an opportunity to look at a variety of ways of producing shapes using squares. Encourage the children to think closely about obscure shapes as well as more regular arrays such as those on the photocopiable sheet.

## Review

- Review the ideas and results and discuss the children's thoughts, particularly if pairs differ in their answers.
- Ask the children to look at the shapes and discuss the key elements (the shape of the playground and the number of mobile classrooms). Compare these with more obscure irregular shapes.

### Next steps

- Ask the children to continue to investigate the patterns of odd and even grids. Maps could be used and street grids (of some towns) could be looked at in comparison. Some of the children might be able to use their ideas to predict how many policemen might be needed for a certain sized street grid.

# Dinner ladies

A dinner lady is on duty at lunchtime in the playground. She must be able to see in all directions around the playground.

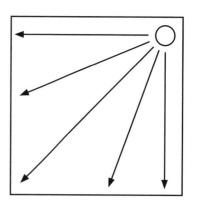

There are some new mobile classrooms at the school. A dinner lady must stand at the corner of the classroom to see two sides of the classroom. Therefore two dinner ladies are needed – one on each corner – to see around this classroom.

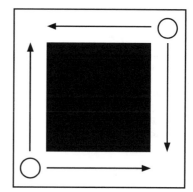

◼ What is the smallest number of dinner ladies needed to see around these extra mobile classrooms?

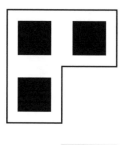  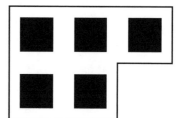

 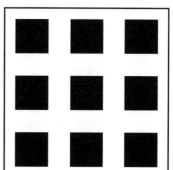

◼ Investigate different groups of mobile classrooms.

# Counterton map

## Activity introduction

- Introduce the activity by showing a plan of your classroom, perhaps using an interactive whiteboard. Draw the compass key and (if necessary) explain the compass directions and how you know which way is north in the classroom.
- Read out the statements on your prepared clue cards (see 'You will need' left), asking the children where on the plan each item should be placed. Draw the items on the plan, using the appropriate colour and building a key as you go. For example:

### 2G Classroom map

| | | | D | | | | Key: | |
|---|---|---|---|---|---|---|---|---|
| | | T | | | | | D | Door |
| | T | | | T | | | T | Table block |
| D | | T | T | | | | S | Sink |
| | | S | TD | D | | | TD | Teacher's desk |

- Discuss any difficulties the children may have had processing the information on the clue cards.

## Activity development

- Provide each group with some coloured counters (red, yellow, blue, green, black and white), together with the map and set of clue cards from photocopiable page 95. Ideally, the children should be divided into groups of two, three or six, so that they have an equal number of cards to read out to each other.
- Emphasise that they must all read out their instructions carefully to the rest of the group and must not show their cards to the others (this will help to ensure that everyone participates).
- Ask the children to read the cards carefully and work together to lay the counters on the map. When they have completed the task, ask appropriate questions relating to any difficulties they may have had and how well their group worked together.

## Review

- Review the task and the strategies used to work out the solution, and discuss any questions posed by the children.
- To take the ideas further, tell the children that they must work out which is your favourite shop by asking questions with only a 'yes' or 'no' answer. For example: *Is your favourite shop north of the school?*

### Learning objectives
**(Y2) Shape strand:** Follow and give instructions involving position, direction and movement.
**(Y3) Use/apply strand:** Follow a line of enquiry by deciding what information is important.
**(Y3) Shape strand:** Read and record the vocabulary of position, direction and movement, using the four compass directions to describe movement about a grid.

### Expected prior knowledge
- Work collaboratively in a group and make group decisions.
- Recognise the four compass directions.

### You will need
Interactive whiteboard (optional); coloured whiteboard/marker pens; plan of your classroom; a range of colour-coded clue cards bearing statements relating to items in your classroom (for example: *the sink is in the south of the classroom and is white*); map and set of laminated clue cards from photocopiable page 95 (one set per pair/group); coloured counters; large squared paper (optional).

### Key vocabulary
map, direction, north, south, east, west

### Brainteaser link
8: 'Is it true? (1)' on page 13.

### Next steps
- Provide the children with blank cards so that they can to make up their own clues. They could set up a similar problem to the one on photocopiable page 95, but with different colours, or they could write a set of clues that will lead the solver to some ancient town treasure.
- Encourage the children to draw their own maps on large squared paper (2cm × 2cm or 3cm × 3cm squares), making up clues to go with them. Asking them to draw a map with a similar structure to that of Counterton will give a familiar structure to this open-ended task.

# Counterton map

## Great North Road

| H | H | N |
|---|---|---|
| | | H |
| | | H |
| H | H | S |

| L | | H | | H | | H |
|---|---|---|---|---|---|---|
| H | | | | | | |
| H | | | | | | |
| Supermarket | | S | S | H | H | |

**West End Lane**

### The High Street

| H | H | S |
|---|---|---|
| | | S |
| | | S |
| Swimming Pool | | N |

**Market Square**

**East Street**

| School | |
|---|---|
| H | |
| H | |
| S | S |

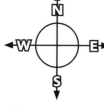

**Key:**
H House
S Shop
N Newsagent
L Library

### South Street

---

| There are three black shops that are north of the High Street. All the other shops are red. | The newsagent on the corner of West End Lane and Great North Road is yellow. The other newsagent is green. |
|---|---|
| There are four blue houses in Counterton. | All the houses on East Street and the High Street are white. |
| The house next to the supermarket is blue. | There are five yellow houses on the road that has the library on it. The library is green. |

# Cube puzzle

## Activity introduction
● Using a large whiteboard or an interactive whiteboard, present a simple enlarged cross as below:

● Ask the children to discuss with a partner how they might describe this shape. Gather ideas and discuss the properties of the shape, resolving any misconceptions.
● Establish what a mirror line is and how you might find out if this shape has one (if not already discussed). Identify all four mirror lines.
● Interactive whiteboard tools can be used to select four areas of the cross (as below), which can be cut and pasted into different areas on the board. If an interactive whiteboard is not available, use an ordinary whiteboard with coloured pens instead.

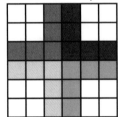

● Discuss the pieces as shown above and relate these to the mirror lines. Ask the children to think what else they might know about these 'cut' pieces. If they allude to rotational symmetry, discuss this concept with them.
● Ask the children how else they might cut the cross into four pieces. Allow them thinking time, then gather their ideas, illustrate them on the board and discuss the results.

## Activity development
● Provide each child with photocopiable page 97 and a pair of scissors. Ask them to cut out the shapes from the page.
● Talk through the task and ask the children to follow the questions on the sheet. Offer large squared paper so that they can develop their ideas further by either colouring shapes or cutting them out.
● Ask the children to think about the shapes they are making. Can they identify the mirror lines of any shapes that are symmetrical?

## Review
● Review the children's ideas and the shapes created from the cross. Discuss the mirror lines and symmetry of their new shape pieces.

### Next steps
● Encourage the children to make their own 'shape puzzles' using squared paper and/or card. Working in pairs, they could prepare a puzzle for the class.

# Cube puzzle

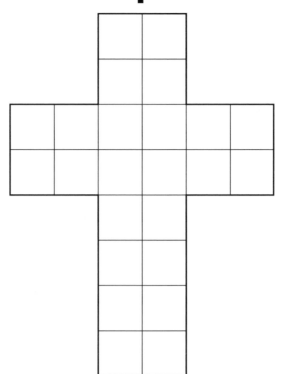

◾ Cut out the shapes below and arrange them to form a cross (as above).

◾ What do you notice about the number and types of shape? Are any the same? Or are they all different?

◾ Make your own puzzle using the cross. There are five pieces in this puzzle – make a puzzle using a different number of pieces.

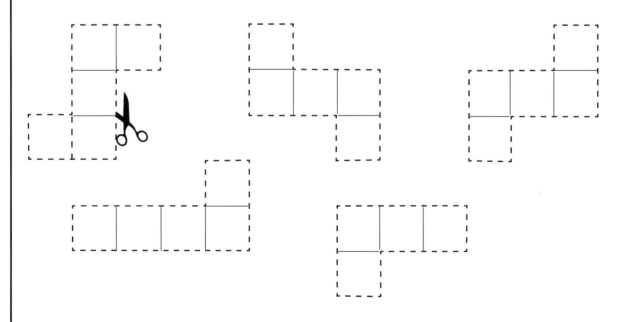

# Shape double

## Learning objectives
(Y2) Use/apply strand:
Follow a line of enquiry;
answer questions by
choosing and using suitable
equipment and selecting,
organising and presenting
information.
(Y2) Measure strand:
Estimate, compare and
measure lengths... using
standard units.

## Expected prior knowledge
● Understand perimeter as
the distance around the
outside edge of a shape.
● Understand and use the
term 'double'.

## You will need
Photocopiable page 99; pre-
cut small and large squares,
triangles and rectangles
matching the dimensions on
the sheet (allow four small
shapes for every large
shape); squared paper.

## Key vocabulary
perimeter, area, double

## Brainteaser links
8: 'Is it true? (1)' on page
13.
13: 'Shoe size' on page 15.

## Activity introduction

● Hand out copies of photocopiable page 99 to each child. Invite the children to measure the perimeter of the small and large square. Ask: *What do you notice?* Establish that the perimeter of the large square is twice that of the small square.
● Ask the children to estimate how many of the small squares will cover the large square. Then ask them to test their prediction. Ask: *What is being measured when you covered the large squares with smaller squares?*
● Establish that area is the amount of space that the shape occupies and that this can be measured by covering the shape.
● Discuss the difference between area and perimeter. Establish that the perimeter is the distance around the outside of the shape and the area is the amount of space inside. The analogy of a field with a fence surrounding it may be a useful where the fence is the perimeter and the area is the grass.
● Establish that the area of the large square is four times the area of the smaller square and that the perimeter of the large square is twice that of the small square.

## Activity development

● Allow the children to work through the remainder of photocopiable page 99 independently to investigate the perimeter and area of the triangle and rectangle. Establish that for each shape, when the perimeter is doubled, the area is multiplied by four.
● This activity allows children to discover a relationship between area and perimeter. If the dimensions of the perimeter are doubled, this will result in an area four times as big. This is true for any polygon. Discovering relationships and identifying connections are central to successful development in mathematics.

## Review

● Share findings. Present the children with a large and small hexagon, where again the perimeter of the large hexagon is twice that of the smaller.
● Ask: *Do you think the area of the large hexagon is four times that of the small hexagon? How can we test out our prediction?*
● The small hexagons do not fit neatly inside the large hexagon. Three hexagons can remain whole but the fourth needs to be cut in order for it to fit.

### Next steps
● Ask the children to investigate other shapes. They can use squared paper to draw other squares and rectangles and then these can be cut out.

# Shape double

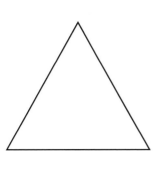

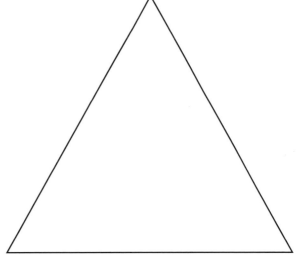

# Go fishing

## Learning objectives
**(Y2) Use/apply strand:** Solve problems involving addition, subtraction, multiplication or division in contexts of numbers.
**(Y2) Measure strand:** Estimate, compare and measure lengths... using standard units and suitable measuring instruments.

## Expected prior knowledge
● Measure in centimetres.
● Know the number bonds to 20.

## You will need
Image of 20cm fish from photocopiable page 101, copied onto card (one per child); 30cm rulers; photocopiable page 101 (one per pair); number lines (optional); metre sticks.

## Key vocabulary
measure, estimate, metre, centimetre

## Brainteaser link
13: 'Shoe size' on page 15.

## Activity introduction
● Begin by handing out copies of the image of the 20cm fish from photocopiable page 101. Ask: *How long is the fish? Can you estimate its length? How can you measure its length?*
● After they have estimated, allow the children to use rulers to measure the length of the fish. Establish that it is 20cm.
● Now provide each pair of children with a copy of photocopiable page 101 and introduce the problem. Ask: *If one of the fish (the one we have just measured) is 20cm and in total all three fish measure 40cm, are the other two fish longer or shorter than this one? What is the total length of the other two fish? If they were the same lengths, what length would they be?*
● State that the other two fish are in fact different lengths. Ask: *What lengths could they be?* Take one of the children's suggestion and record it on the board.
● Ask: *Is this the only answer?* Then direct the children to investigate and find as many solutions as they can.

## Activity development
● A ruler or number line may support the children in investigating and finding pairs of numbers that total 20. Encourage them to record their work so that they are able to share their findings in the review session.

## Review
● Collect the children's findings and then show them how these findings may be presented in a systematic way that enables them to check whether they have found all the possibilities. For example:

| First fish (cm) | Second fish (cm) |
|---|---|
| 19 | 1 |
| 18 | 2 |
| 17 | 3 |
| 16 | 4 |

● Recording in this manner enables children to see patterns and relationships between the numbers. They should be encouraged to link the patterns of bonds to 10 with bonds to 20 (for example, 9 + 1 = 10 and 19 + 1 = 20).

### Next steps
● The above activity can be extended by asking the children to calculate the length of all three fish.

# Go fishing

The fisherman catches three fish. He measures their length. In total they measure 40cm.

◗ How long could each fish be?

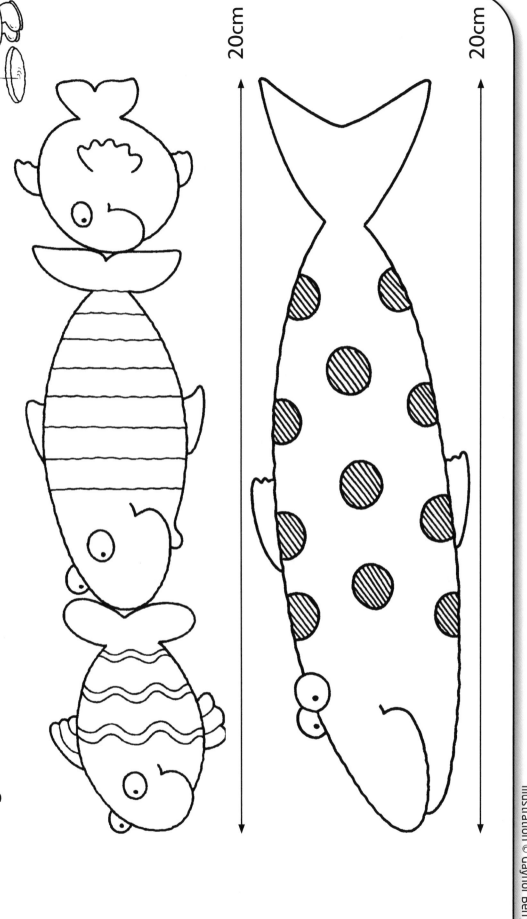

20cm

20cm

# Ribbons

## Learning objectives
(Y1) Use/apply strand:
Answer a question by selecting and using suitable equipment, and sorting information, shapes or objects.
(Y2) Measure strand:
Estimate, compare and measure lengths... using standard units.

## Expected prior knowledge
● Use logic and reasoning skills to solve problems.
● Use a ruler to measure in centimetres.

## You will need
Photocopiable page 103 (one per pair); scissors; strips of paper approx 2cm x 20cm (six per pair); 30cm rulers.

## Key vocabulary
long, short, longer, shorter, longest, shortest, centimetre, measure

## Brainteaser link
15: 'Clothes size' on page 16.

## Activity introduction
● Introduce the children to the problem on photocopiable page 103 (finding the length of each piece of ribbon) and together read the clue cards. Ask: *How can these clues help us to solve the problem?*
● Encourage the children to realise that the cards give us clues to solve the problem, but that we need to use all of them to ensure that we get to the correct answer.
● Read out and discuss the clue card 'The pink is the shortest'. Ask: *What information does this card give? How can we use it to solve the problem?*
● Hand out copies of photocopiable page 103 to each pair of children and ask them to cut out a set of cards. Explain that this will enable them to move the cards around, which will help to solve the problem.

## Activity development
● After the cards have been cut out, let the children work in pairs to put the colour cards in order by using the clue cards.
● Ask: *How do you know they are in the correct order?* Encourage each pair to explain their reasoning and justify their solution. Ask: *What then is the length of each ribbon?*
● Having established the length of each ribbon, the children then measure and cut a strip of paper to represent each ribbon and label each with appropriate length.

## Solution

| | |
|---|---|
| Pink 10cm | Red 12cm |
| Yellow 15cm | Green 16cm |
| Black 18cm | Blue 20cm |

● This problem cannot be solved in one step but needs to be worked through by looking at each clue and using them in combination. Sometimes a clue will need to be put to one side and returned to later.
● Do not give children too much support, particularly at the beginning of the task.

## Review
● Display a set of cut strips in the form of a bar chart. Ask: *How many ribbons are longer than 13cm? How much longer than the blue ribbon is the green ribbon? How much shorter than the yellow ribbon is the pink ribbon? If the pink and the red ribbon were placed end to end, how many centimetres would it measure? Can you find two ribbons that together measure 30cm?*

### Next steps
● Encourage the children to create their own problem for others to solve. Explain that they should write the solution first (for example, red is 5cm, yellow is 7cm, blue is 8cm and brown is 10cm) and then write the clues for putting them in order.

# Ribbons

There are six ribbons, each a different colour and length. The ribbons measure 10cm, 12cm, 15cm, 16cm, 18cm and 20cm.

🫧 Use the clues below to put the ribbons in order and find the length of each.

| | |
|---|---|
| Black | Pink |
| Red | Green |
| Yellow | Blue |

| | |
|---|---|
| The black is longer than the green. | The blue is longer than the yellow. |
| The black is not the longest. | The yellow is between the red and the green. |
| The red is shorter than the green. | The pink is the shortest. |

# The hungry bug

## Activity introduction
● Ask the children to pass around and hold the 1kg and 1g mass and talk about which is the heaviest and which is the lightest.
● Ask: *How much heavier than the gram is the kilogram?* Establish that the kilogram mass is 1000 times heavier than the gram mass.
● Pass around some leaves. Ask the children to estimate how heavy they are. Establish that they are no more than a few grams each. They are nearer to the mass of the gram than the kilogram.
● Ask: *If a caterpillar ate three leaves and these leaves weighed three grams in total, what was the weight of each leaf?* Collect solutions and establish that there are several possible alternatives.

## Activity development
● Introduce the children to the problem on photocopiable page 105 and allow them to investigate. Remind them that they may be able to find more than one answer for each day.

## Solution

| Day | 1g | 3g | 5g | 7g | |
|---|---|---|---|---|---|
| Monday | 1 | 1 | | | = 4g |
| Tuesday | | | | 1 | = 7g |
| Wednesday | | | 2 | | = 10g |
| Wednesday | | 1 | | 1 | = 10g |
| Thursday | | 1 | 2 | | = 13g |
| Thursday | | 2 | | 1 | = 13g |
| Friday | 1 | | 3 | | = 16g |
| Friday | | 3 | | 1 | = 16g |
| Saturday | | | 4 | | = 20g |
| Saturday | | 2 | | 2 | = 20g |

● Alternative solutions are shown in the above table for the minimum number of leaves.

## Review
● Briefly share some of the children's solutions. Ask: *What was the minimum number of leaves Billy the bug could have eaten on each day?*
● Ask: *On Sunday Billy ate 100 grams. Which leaves did he eat?* Encourage the children to use multiples of 10 as an easy solution (for example 10 × 7g + 10 × 3g = 100g).

### Next steps
● The above activity involves working with number in the context of grams. It should be emphasised that working with grams is not significantly different from working with number in other contexts. The same rules of arithmetic apply.
● Both grams and kilograms were introduced in the activity. It is important that children develop an understanding of the relationship between the two and have some practical appreciation of their mass.
● A useful activity is for children to identify objects that weigh more than 1kg and those that are less. Practical exploration is important in order for children to be able to estimate an object's mass. Allow a wide range of estimates.

**Learning objectives**
(Y2) Use/apply strand:
Solve problems involving addition.
(Y2) Measure strand:
Estimate, compare and measure lengths, weights and capacities, choosing and using standard units (m, cm, kg, litre).

**Expected prior knowledge**
● Use mental calculation strategies to add single digit numbers.

**You will need**
1kg mass; 1g mass; a collection of leaves; photocopiable page 105.

**Key vocabulary**
grams, kilograms

**Brainteaser link**
13: 'Shoe size' on page 15.

Name _____

# The hungry bug

Billy the bug eats leaves.

On Monday he ate 4 grams.

On Tuesday he ate 7 grams.

On Wednesday he ate 10 grams.

On Thursday he ate 13 grams.

On Friday he ate 16 grams.

On Saturday he ate 20 grams.

▪ Identify which leaves Billy ate on each day. There may be more than one answer for each day.

Illustration © Gaynor Berry

# Tetrominoes

## Learning objectives
**(Y2) Use/apply strand:**
Describe patterns and relationships involving numbers or shapes, make predictions and test these with examples.
**(Y2) Shape strand:**
Visualise common 2D shapes and 3D solids; identify shapes from pictures of them in different positions and orientations; sort, make and describe shapes, referring to their properties.

## Expected prior knowledge
● Investigate and persevere with an activity.

## You will need
Sufficient Multilink™ for each child/pair to make two of each of the tetrominoes (each type of tetromino should have its own unique colour so that it can be identified when the shapes are combined); photocopiable page 107; squared paper; coloured pencils.

## Key vocabulary
T shape, L shape, rectangle, z shape, square

## Brainteaser links
6: 'Crack the code' on page 13.
19: 'Rough snack symmetry' on page 17.

## Activity introduction
● Tell each child to take four cubes of one colour and join them to make a shape. Invite them to describe their shape using both everyday and mathematical language. Ask: *How many faces does it have? How many edges does it have?*
● Ask the children to focus on just one face of their 3D shape and imagine that this face was just a 2D shape. Ask: *How many sides does it have?*

## Activity development
● Introduce photocopiable page 107 and ask the children if they can place their shape so that it fits one of the drawn spaces on the photocopiable page. They may have to turn it around or over so that it is the same orientation.
● Ask the children to make two of each of the shapes on the sheet from cubes using the stated colour.
● Once the shapes have been constructed, ask the children to select four of their ten shapes and place them in the grid to create a square. Ask: *How many different squares can you make?* Let them record their solutions on squared paper using coloured pencils.
● Encourage the children to reason and understand that a shape is the same even though it might be in a different orientation.

## Review
● Ask one child (or pair of children) to share a solution. How many other children have the same solution? Remind them that they may have the same solution but it may look different as it is in a different position. A good check is first to identify if the same shapes have been used (for example, two rectangles and two squares as in shape 1 below) and then to check if the same shapes are next to each other (the two squares are in the middle and the two rectangles are on the outside).
● Quickly make the square and then turn it around so that the children can see it presented in different orientations.
● Repeat this for each solution, making the square each time to keep as a record. You can use the children's ready-made tetrominoes to construct the squares. It is unlikely that children will have identified all 15 of the squares in one lesson. The identified squares can be left on display and added to as the children identify others.

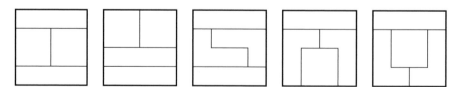

> ## Next steps
> ● A similar activity can be carried out using pentominoes (five squares). The children can first investigate how many different pentominoes there are (12) and then investigate making different rectangles from them (they will not find all of them as there are many solutions).

# Tetrominoes

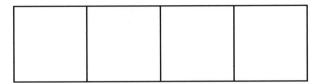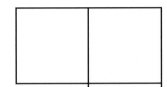

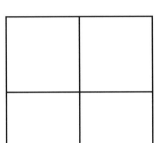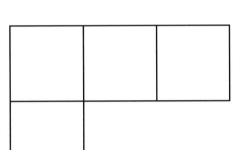

◼ Place four of the shapes in the grid below to make a square.

◼ How many different squares can you make?

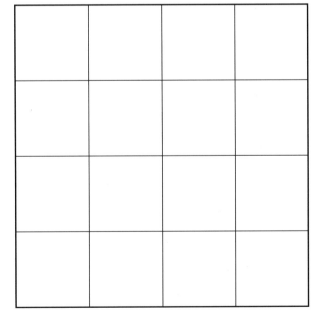

# Bedtime

**Learning objectives**
**(Y2) Use/apply strand:**
Solve problems involving addition, subtraction, multiplication or division.
**(Y2) Measure strand:** Use units of time (seconds, minutes, hours, days) and know the relationships between them; read the time to the quarter hour; identify time intervals, including those that cross the hour.

**Expected prior knowledge**
● Display a knowledge of hours and minutes.

**You will need**
Photocopiable page 109 (one per child/pair); a demonstration clock; individual clocks; blank number lines.

**Key vocabulary**
hours, minutes, time

## Activity introduction
● Discuss the time taken to complete activities that the children are involved in between getting home from school and bedtime. For example: having tea/dinner, playing outside, looking after pets, watching TV.
● Ask: *If Jack started eating his tea at 5 o'clock and took 20 minutes, at what time did he finish?* Let the children work in pairs, where one child shows the starting time and the other shows the finishing time.
● Ask: *Jack then watched a TV programme for 30 minutes. At what time did it finish?* Ask the children to show the time on their clocks.
● Repeat the activity with events starting at different times.

## Activity development
● Introduce photocopiable page 109 to the children. Ask: *What activities does Harry have to complete before bedtime? How long does he have to complete these activities?* Establish that Harry has exactly one hour to complete the four activities.
● There are many different combinations of time that total one hour. However, you should encourage the children to give reasonable answers. For example, one minute to read a book is not plausible!
● The children may use their clocks to support their calculations or alternatively they may use a blank number line, which can be a powerful tool for the addition of time and should be modelled to illustrate its use:

For example:     Tidy toys: 10 minutes
                          Feed the guinea pig: 20 minutes
                          Get changed and clean teeth: 10 minutes
                          Read book: 20 minutes
                          Total: 60 minutes
can be modelled on the number line below:

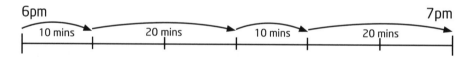

6pm                                                                                     7pm

| 10 mins | 20 mins | 10 mins | 20 mins |

● When the children have found one solution, ask them to find another.

## Review
● Share some alternative solutions and check them by counting up each time around a clock face and then along a number line.
● Ask: *If each activity took the same length of time, how long would each take?*

**Next steps**
● Time can often be an area which children, including more able learners, take a long time to grasp. To support development, provide as many opportunities as possible to discuss time as part of everyday activities.

# Bedtime

Harry goes to bed at 7 o'clock.
At 6 o'clock he had to:
    tidy his toys
    feed the guinea pig
    get changed and clean his teeth
    read his book.

◀ How long did he spend on each activity?

_____

_____

_____

_____

Illustration © Gaynor Berry

# Equi-match dominoes

## Learning objectives
**(Y1) Measure strand:** Estimate, measure, weigh and compare objects, choosing and using suitable standard units and measuring instruments.
**(Y2) Measure strand:** Estimate, compare and measure lengths, weights and capacities, choosing and using standard units.
**(Y3) Measure strand:** Know the relationships between kilometres and metres, metres and centimetres, kilograms and grams, litres and millilitres.

## Expected prior knowledge
● Know that we measure our height and distance in mm, cm or km.
● Know that we measure flour or sugar in kilograms.
● Know that we measure our milk (or drinks) in litres.

## You will need
Enlarged set of dominoes from photocopiable page 111; prepared dominoes, copied onto card from photocopiable page 111 and laminated (one set per pair).

## Key vocabulary
measure, standard units, length, capacity, mass, kilograms, grams, millilitres, litres, millimetres, metres, kilometres

## Brainteaser links
13: 'Shoe size' on page 15.
15: 'Clothes size' on page 16.

## Activity introduction
● This activity reinforces the correct use of vocabulary in relation to the equivalence of standard measuring units. Stack the enlarged set of dominoes made from photocopiable page 111 in a pile face down. Turn the top card over and show the children what is on the card.
● Discuss what the pictures might represent and what the unit measurements shown mean.
● Ask questions about equivalents. For example, for the 1 litre card, ask: *What is 1 litre in millilitres?* If the card shows the word 'length', ask: *What units do we use to measure length?* Encourage individuals to declare what they already know.
● Turn over another card and ask if any of the words match or have a connection with any of the words on the first card. Display the second card where it matches, or leave it aside to use later.
● Continue to match the cards at one end or the other.
● Provide each pair of children with a set of dominoes from photocopiable page 111 and describe the rules you wish to apply. There are several different ways to play dominoes, including: (a) Choose five cards each and take turns to lay down a card; (b) If you cannot lay a card down, pick another card from the pile and wait until it is your turn again; (c) Challenge each pair to place all their domino cards correctly as quickly as possible.

## Activity development
● Using the same domino cards, encourage the children to play other games to reinforce these equivalences.
● Snap: Share out the domino cards between each player. Take turns to lay a card down on top each other. When two consecutive cards match either end of the domino, call 'SNAP'. The first child to call keeps the pile. At the end of the game the child who has the most cards wins.
● Stop the clock: Place all the cards from one set in a pile face down. Take it in turns to turn over the top card and identify the equivalent units and what they are used to measure as appropriate. For example, for the card 'Capacity/1000mm' the child must identify capacity as the measure of liquid/milk/cola and state that 1000mm is equal to 1m. If they are correct, they can keep the card and turn the next card over. This game can be played against the clock.

## Review
● Review the different times that may have been recorded in the card games.
● Discuss what makes some matches easier than others.

### Next steps
● Investigate the value for money of different food and drink items (such as fizzy drinks, juices and so on).
● Ask: *How tall is our class/table/group?* Involve the children in measuring everyone in the class/table/group and add the heights together.

# Equi-match dominoes

| | | | | |
|---|---|---|---|---|
| 1000ml  · I kilo  | 1000g 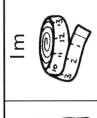 · Im 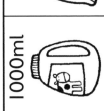 | Kilometre  · Mass  | 1000m  · IL 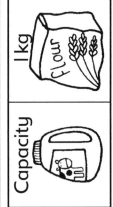 | Capacity  · Ikg 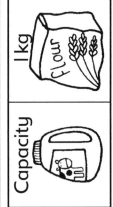 |
| 1000g  · I litre  | 1000ml  · I metre  | Mass 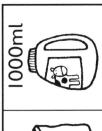 · 1000ml  | Capacity  · 1000mm  | 1000mm  · I litre  |
| Mass  · I metre  | Length  · 1000g  | Ikg 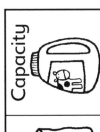 · Capacity  | I litre  · Length  | 1000mm  · A kilogram 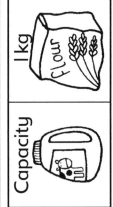 |

# Dates, days and months

**Learning objectives**
**(Y1) Measure strand:** Use vocabulary related to time; order days of the week and months.
**(Y2) Measure strand:** Use units of time and know the relationships between them.
**(Y3) Measure strand:** Calculate time intervals and find start or end times for a given time interval.

**Expected prior knowledge**
● Recall that there are seven days in a week and twelve months in a year.

**You will need**
Photocopiable page 113 (one per child); current calendar (one per pair); school calendar listing the last day of term; a range of other calendars (calendars set out in a different way, calendars from other years, calendars listing important dates in the school year).

**Key vocabulary**
dates, days, week, month, year, pattern, gaps, relationship

## Activity introduction
● Write out the poem '30 days has September' on the board for all the class to see. Read the poem aloud and ask appropriate questions, such as: *Which is the shortest month of the year? How many days do the longest months have?*
● Identify when selected children in the class have their birthday and record their names against the month in the poem.
● To emphasise how to count across months, use examples of birthdays in adjacent months. Establish that these birthdays might be separated by only two or three days.

## Activity development
● Provide each child with photocopiable page 113 and each pair of children with a copy of this year's calendar.
● Discuss the questions on the sheet and ensure that they are understood. Children should work on these questions in pairs or groups.
● When the children have completed all the questions, ask them to look carefully at the calendar page for this month, which they have constructed on the photocopiable page. Ask them to look for patterns in the numbers (for example, they should realise that Friday can be calculated by adding on 7 each time). You may want to look at a page of calendars so that the children can see clearly the adjacent months.
● Ask the children to make up their own questions using the patterns and relationships they have discovered For example: *If the first Tuesday in June is the 11th, what date will the second Tuesday be?*
● Provide the children with copies of other calendars. These could include current calendars that are set out in different ways and calendars from previous years. Ask the children to explain what the differences are.

## Review
● Review the task and select a range of questions posed by the children. Discuss the answers and the strategies used to work them out.

### Next steps
● To extend the children's understanding of patterns with consecutive numbers, offer them a grid (for example, a 5 × 5 grid or a 100-square). Ask them to look at a block of numbers and see if they notice anything about the sum of the diagonals (they are equal; for example, in the shaded block below 7 + 13 = 20 and 8 + 12 = 20):

| 1 | 2 | 3 | 4 | 5 |
|---|---|---|---|---|
| 6 | 7 | 8 | 9 | 10 |
| 11 | 12 | 13 | 14 | 15 |
| 16 | 17 | 18 | 19 | 20 |
| 21 | 22 | 23 | 24 | 25 |

● Ask: *Is this true for all blocks of squares in this grid? Why?* Discuss the relationships between consecutive numbers and the position of numbers in the grid.

# Dates, days and months

| | | | | | |
|---|---|---|---|---|---|
| S | | | | | |
| M | | | | | |
| T | | | | | |
| W | | | | | |
| Th | | | | | |
| F | | | | | |
| Sat | | | | | |

◼ What is the day and date today? Write the date in the correct box on the calendar grid above.

◼ Now complete the calendar grid working forward/backward from today's date.

◼ Find the month of your birthday in a calendar.

◼ How many days are in your birthday month?

◼ How many days are there in this month?

◼ How many days are there until the end of this month (from today)?

◼ What was the date last Saturday?

◼ On what day will the first day of next month be?

◼ Using the school's calendar, what day is the end of term?

◼ Make up six new questions about the calendar to ask your partner.

◼ Can you think of a calendar question for your teacher?

# Vegetable plot

## Learning objectives
**(Y2) Use/apply strand:**
Solve problems involving addition, subtraction, multiplication or division in contexts of numbers [and] measures.
**(Y2) Measure strand:** Estimate, compare and measure lengths, choosing and using standard units.
**(Y3) Measure strand:** Know the relationships between... metres and centimetres.

## Expected prior knowledge
● Know that a metre is a measurement of length.
● Know that there are 100 centimetres in a metre.

## You will need
Photocopiable page 115 (one per pair); squared paper; rulers and pencils; coloured pencils (optional); pictures of vegetables or real vegetables (optional).

## Key vocabulary
metre, centimetres, divide, multiply

## Brainteaser link
13: 'Shoe size' on page 15.

## Activity introduction
● Introduce the idea of a vegetable plot. Ask: *What is a vegetable patch? Why do people have them in their gardens? What size are they?*
● Ask if any children have their own patch of garden at home and discuss what they grow. Ask/discuss why many vegetables are planted in rows and talk about the space needed for the vegetables to grow.
● On the board, draw a scaled rectangle of 1 × 2 metres. Explain that you want to plant a total of 18 potato plants in your plot, highlighting that ideally potatoes need to grow 30cm apart.
● Ask the children to discuss with their partners how they might plant 18 potato plants in the plot. Emphasise that changing the metres to centimetres can help to work out a planting scheme. Suppose the potatoes can be planted near to the edge - does this make a difference to the planting scheme? One solution is:

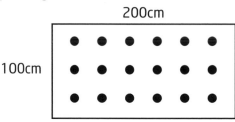

200cm

100cm

● It might be helpful to look at a picture of a potato plant (from the internet or a book) and discuss the space potatoes need. There is an opportunity to make a link with art (for example, the children could construct their own potato plant using wire and papier mâché, or make a picture out of green tissue paper to get a feel of how wide 30cm is). Ask how high the plants might grow (this varies according to variety, but a good estimate would be approximately 50cm high).
● Gather the children's ideas and discuss as appropriate.

## Activity development
● Provide the children with photocopiable page 115 and squared paper to help them in their calculations. Discuss how they might start to solve the problem on the sheet.
● Pictures (or actual examples) of what the plants listed on page 115 look like in the ground might be helpful for some children.
● Offer thinking time and gather ideas before the children begin the task. Guide them in how you want their thinking and work recorded. One option is to use squared paper and shade squares (representing the different vegetables) with coloured pencils. Tally charts, bar charts, pictograms and other types of graph or chart are also possibilities.

## Review
● Review the children's ideas and compare layouts with a large number of plants and those with less vegetables in total but a more even balance of the different types. Discuss the results.

### Next steps
● Move on to the extension question on photocopiable page 115 and ask the children to record their calculations carefully.

# Vegetable plot

Mrs Collins' vegetable plot is only 1 metre wide by 5 metres long. She wants to grow some of the following vegetables:

    Broad beans must be planted 20cm apart.
    Beetroot must be planted 10cm apart.
    Carrots must be planted 10cm apart.
    Potatoes must be planted 30cm apart.

◢ Help Mrs Collins plan her vegetable plot. Begin by drawing the plot on squared paper.

◢ How many of each vegetable can Mrs Collins plant in the plot?

◢ Is this the most vegetables you can plant in a plot of this size?

## Extension

◢ What if Mrs Collins wanted to plant these vegetables too? How many could she squeeze in?

    Radish must be planted 5cm apart.
    Onions must be planted 5cm apart.
    Lettuce must be planted 20cm apart.

Illustration © Gaynor Berry

# Flower garden

**Learning objectives**
**(Y1) Use/apply strand:**
Solve problems involving counting, adding, subtracting, doubling or halving in the context of numbers.
**(Y1) Data strand:** Use diagrams to sort objects into groups according to a given criterion; suggest a different criterion for grouping the same objects.

**Expected prior knowledge**
● Divide objects into equal groups.

**You will need**
Photocopiable page 117 (one per child); pots of counters to represent flowers (enough for 18 counters per child).

**Key vocabulary**
row, column, total

**Brainteaser link**
3: 'Make 12' on page 12.

## Activity introduction
● Introduce photocopiable page 117 to the children, and explain the first problem. Ask: *How many flowers are there altogether? What strategy can be used for counting them?* Encourage alternative strategies to counting in ones.
● Ask: *How many flowers each will Mary and her three brothers have?* If the children are struggling, ask: *If they each had five, would there be a total of 40?* Establish that 5 will not work, so encourage them to try out other solutions until the correct one is found (ten flowers each).
● Ask: *How can the flowers be divided into four equal sections?* Point out that one way is to divide them into four columns, as on the photocopiable page. Ask the children to check that this works, that there are ten flowers in each column. The next obvious solution is to investigate whether dividing into rows works.
● Encourage the children to find the less obvious solutions, where sections are grouped into blocks. Some of these are illustrated below (alternative combinations of these solutions are also possible).

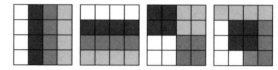

## Activity development
● Introduce the second activity on photocopiable page 117.
● Place pots of counters on the table. Explain that one counter represents one flower.
● Ask the children to take out as many counters as they will need to represent the flowers in the garden. (This should be 18 flowers each.)
● The use of counters will allow for a trial and improvement method as children are able to move the counters around until they find a solution. The most obvious solution is to divide the flowers equally between the nine sections. Encourage the children to find an alternative solution.

## Solutions

| 2 | 2 | 2 |
|---|---|---|
| 2 | 2 | 2 |
| 2 | 2 | 2 |

| 1 | 2 | 3 |
|---|---|---|
| 2 | 3 | 1 |
| 3 | 1 | 2 |

(The second solution may be presented in a different order.)

## Review
● Share the children's solutions with the group. Are the solutions for the second activity all the same? Contrast and compare the different suggestions.

**Next steps**
● This activity can be followed up with brainteaser 3 ('Make 12'), which is a similar activity.

# Flower garden

Mary wants to divide her flower garden into four equal areas so that she and her three brothers have the same number of flowers to look after.

◾ How many flowers will they have each?

_____

◾ How many ways can you find to divide the garden? Here is one way:

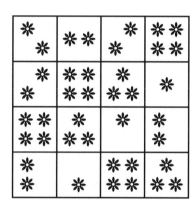 

◾ You have 18 flowers. Plant them in the grid below so that every row and column totals the same number.

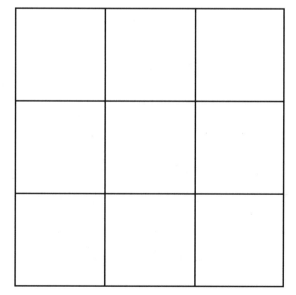

# Domino sort

## Learning objectives
**(Y2) Use/apply strand:**
Follow a line of enquiry;
answer questions by
choosing and using suitable
equipment and selecting,
organising and presenting
information in lists, tables
and simple diagrams.
**(Y2) Data strand:** Use lists,
tables and diagrams to sort
objects; explain choices
using appropriate language,
including 'not'.

## Expected prior knowledge
● Display knowledge of odd
and even numbers.

## You will need
Photocopiable page 119 (or
use a set of real dominoes);
paper; scissors; glue.

## Key vocabulary
odd, even, total, sort, block
graph

## Brainteaser link
14: 'Football kit' on page 15.

## Activity introduction
● Look at a domino together and discuss the number of spots on each
side. Ask: *Does the domino have two even numbers, two odd numbers
or an odd and an even number? How can we spot whether a number on
a domino is odd or even without counting?*
● Invite the children to look at the patterns on the dominoes and notice
that it is easy to see groups of two on the even numbers.
● Look at another domino and encourage the children to recognise
whether the number is odd or even, without counting.

## Activity development
● Introduce photocopiable page 119 and ask the children to cut out the
dominoes. Read through the instructions on the sheet and ensure that
they understand the task.
● Let the children work together in pairs. Encourage them to discuss
the task and share their ideas with their partners.
● Once the children have sorted their dominoes, ask them to stick them
down on a sheet of paper so that they form a block graph, in sets of
dominoes with two even numbers, two odd numbers and an odd and an
even number. Then ask them to look again at their dominoes and add up
each one in the two even numbers set. Ask: *What do you notice?*
Establish that all of the totals are even.
● Ask: *What do you think the totals of the dominoes with two odd
numbers will be?* Do not correct the prediction if the reply is 'odd' but
allow the children to investigate.
● Repeat the activity for the final set of dominoes on the graph (those
with one odd and one even number).

## Review
● Ask the children what they found out when they added the spots on
the dominoes. Can they give an explanation for why the addition of two
even numbers always results in an even number, or why two odd
numbers also results in an even number?
● Ask questions about the completed block graph. *What does the graph
show us? Are there more odd numbers than even numbers on the
graph?*
● The children may not be able to give a precise mathematical
explanation as to why two odd numbers total an even number; however
they may be able to refer to the dominoes and recognise that the two
odd spots can match to make a pair, thus making the total even.

### Next steps
● The opportunity for recognition of odd and even numbers can occur
in a variety of contexts. When carrying out the operation of addition,
ask the children: *Are the numbers odd or even? Do you expect the
answer to be odd or even?*
● Odd and even are just two possible properties of numbers. Many
numbers will have more than one property. Encourage the children to
begin to recognise other properties of numbers such as multiples of 2, 5
and 10. Multiples of 2 and 10 are also even numbers.

# Domino sort

■ Cut out the dominoes and sort them into three groups:
a) Those with two even numbers.
b) Those with two odd numbers.
c) Those with one odd and one even number.

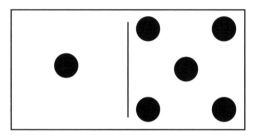
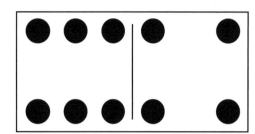

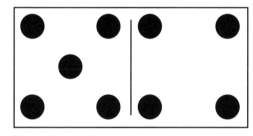
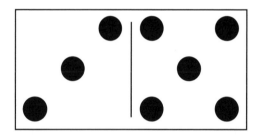

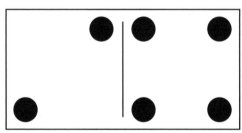
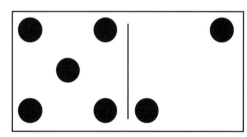

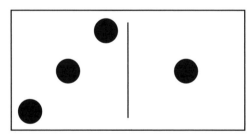
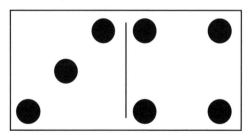

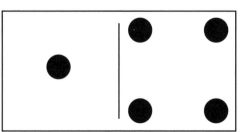
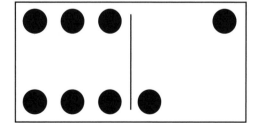

# Train timetable

## Activity introduction
● Begin by counting aloud with the children in steps of 5 minutes, starting at 1 o'clock. Emphasise the need to say '2 o'clock' after 1.55, and not 1.60.
● Ask: *If a train leaves at 10.30 and arrives at 10.50, how long does the journey take?* It may be useful to illustrate the journey on a number line. Repeat with a similar question.
● Show the children the train timetable on an enlarged copy of photocopiable page 121. Ask: *What information does the timetable give us? Why might it be useful to someone?*

## Activity development
● Provide each child with photocopiable page 121. Show them where they need to fill in the missing information. Allow them to work independently on the activity.
● An important skill in this activity is locating the appropriate information to solve the problems. The children may use different strategies for calculating the missing information. The easiest strategy is to add 25 minutes to each of the times from Train 1. However, do allow the children sufficient time to persevere and develop their own strategy. Encourage them to use number lines and informal jottings to support their calculations.

## Solution

|  | Train 1 | | Train 2 | |
| --- | --- | --- | --- | --- |
|  | Arrive | Depart | Arrive | Depart |
| Old Town |  | 10.00 |  | 10.25 |
| Red City | 10.20 | 10.25 | 10.45 | 10.50 |
| Stonebridge | 10.45 | 10.50 | 11.10 | 11.15 |
| Sealport | 10.55 | 11.00 | 11.20 | 11.25 |
| Harrow Hill | 11.15 |  | 11.40 |  |

● Harry's journey from Old Town to Sealport is 55 minutes. Tom's journey from Red City to Harrow Hill is 50 minutes. So Harry's journey is 5 minutes longer.

## Review
● Share solutions and strategies. Ask: *If a train left at 10.40 and arrived at 11.10, how long was the journey?*
● Illustrate bridging through the hour using a number line:

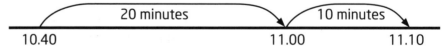

|  | 20 minutes |  | 10 minutes |  |
| --- | --- | --- | --- | --- |
| 10.40 | | 11.00 | | 11.10 |

20 minutes + 10 minutes = 30 minutes.

### Next steps
● Bridging through the hour when calculating time is an important step.
● Children need to appreciate that there are 60 minutes in an hour. This makes calculation different from calculating with just numbers. The number line illustrated above can support calculation.

Name _____

# Train timetable

|  | Train 1 | | Train 2 | |
| --- | --- | --- | --- | --- |
|  | Arrive | Depart | Arrive | Depart |
| Old Town |  | 10.00 |  | 10.25 |
| Red City | 10.20 | 10.25 |  |  |
| Stonebridge | 10.45 | 10.50 |  |  |
| Sealport | 10.55 | 11.00 |  |  |
| Harrow Hill | 11.15 |  |  |  |

◼ Fill in the missing information on the timetable for Train 2, using the timetable information for Train 1.

◼ Harry travels from Old Town to Sealport. Tom travels from Red City to Harrow Hill. Who has the longest journey? How much longer is it?

_____

_____

_Illustration © Gaynor Berry_

# Number sort

## Activity introduction

- Show the children two plastic sorting rings. Label one 'Multiples of 2' and the other 'Less than 10'. Using a set of 1–20 number cards, ask the children to select a number and put it in the appropriate ring. Ask: *Are there any numbers that could go in both rings?*
- Slide the rings together so that there is an intersection. Ask: *What numbers could we put in this middle section? Why do they belong in the middle section?*
- Establish that the overlapping section is part of both circles and so numbers that belong to both sets can go in this section.

## Activity development

- Provide each pair with photocopiable page 123, a set of 1–20 number cards and a pair of scissors. Explain that they should use the large circles at the top of the page to sort the numbers and then use the smaller diagrams to record what they have done.
- Ask the children to cut out the labels from the bottom of the sheet and select any two to label the circles on the large Venn diagram.
- Once the children have labelled their Venn diagram, ask individual pairs: *Which numbers will go in the middle section?* Establish that the answer is numbers which have both properties of the two selected labels.
- Give the children time to sort their numbers. There will be some numbers that cannot go into either of the circles. Explain that these should be placed outside of the circles.
- When the children have finished this first activity, ask them to record their solution in one of the smaller diagrams at the bottom of the sheet.
- Ask them to repeat the activity, using a different pair of labels. Question the children as they work: *Is it possible to put all of the numbers into the two circles? Are there always numbers in the middle section (the intersection)? Which combination of labels allows you to place the most numbers in the circles?*
- There is a variety of solutions and outcomes to the activity. Its value is in giving children the opportunity to reason about numbers and discover relationships between them. For example, the labels 'Odd' and 'Even' do not allow any numbers in the intersection, since there is no number which is both odd and even; the same is true of 'Multiple of 4' and 'Odd' numbers, since multiples of 4 are always even.

## Review

- Share the solutions that the children have recorded on their sheets.
- Ask: *Are there any solutions which do not have any numbers in the middle section? Are there any solutions where all of the numbers placed in the circles are in the middle section? Which two labels had the most numbers within the circles?*

### Next steps

- Ask the children to investigate whether the 2, 4 and 10 times-tables will ever generate odd numbers.

### Learning objectives
**(Y2) Use/apply strand:** Follow a line of enquiry; answer questions by choosing and using suitable equipment and selecting, organising and presenting information in lists, tables and simple diagrams.
**(Y2) Data strand:** Use lists, tables and diagrams to sort objects; explain choices using appropriate language, including 'not'.

### Expected prior knowledge
- Understand properties of number, including odd, even, multiples of 3, multiples of 4 and multiples of 5.

### You will need
Two plastic sorting rings; 1–20 number cards (one set per pair); photocopiable page 123 (one per pair); scissors.

### Key vocabulary
odd, even, multiple, Venn diagram

### Brainteaser link
8: 'Is it true? (1)' on page 13.

Name _____

# Number sort

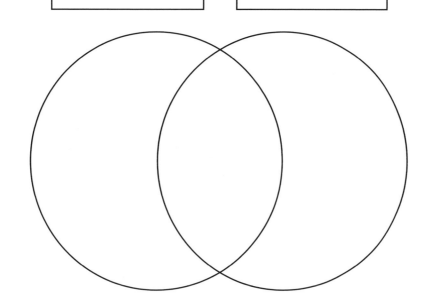

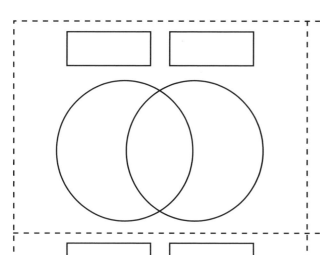

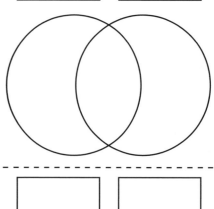

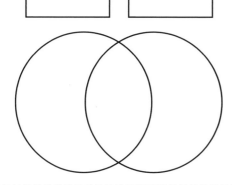

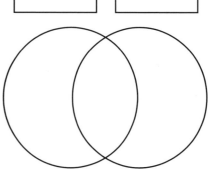

| Odd | Even | Multiple of 3 | Multiple of 4 | Multiple of 5 |

# Wizard hats

## Learning objectives
**(Y1) Use/apply strand:**
Solve problems involving counting.
**(Y1) Use/apply strand:**
Describe ways of solving puzzles and problems, explaining choices and decisions orally or using pictures.
**(Y2) Use/apply strand:**
Identify and record the information or calculation needed to solve a puzzle or problem; carry out the steps or calculations and check the solution in the context of the problem.
**(Y2) Use/apply strand:**
Present solutions to puzzles and problems in an organised way; explain decisions, methods and results in pictorial, spoken or written form, using mathematical language and number sentences.

## You will need
Three shoes (of different colours) or interactive whiteboard; photocopiable page 125 (one per child); linking cubes (optional); squared paper and colouring pens/pencils (optional).

## Expected prior knowledge
● Sort and manipulate objects to solve problems.
● Explain the thinking and understanding behind the solution to a problem.

## Key vocabulary
pattern, systematic, order, present, list, record, organise

## Activity introduction
● Display three different shoes on a table (preferably of noticeably different colours). Explain to the children that you are a shopkeeper and you want to display your shoes differently in the window. Alternatively, use clipart on an interactive whiteboard.
● Ask the children to change the display. They may suggest laying down the shoes in a different ordere, or facing them in different directions. Explore these ideas, encouraging the children to think about the best way of displaying a shoe.
● The aim is to discuss the different orders in which they might be displayed (for example: red shoe, green shoe, brown shoe; brown shoe, red shoe, green shoe). Ask: *In how many ways can the shoes be placed in the window?* Encourage the children to think about this problem in pairs, then gather ideas. (It is not necessary to find an answer at this stage, as you will be returning to the problem again later.)
● Provide each child with photocopiable page 125 and introduce the task. Discuss with the children how they might tackle the activity and how they will know if they have covered all the possibilities.
● Gather ideas of how they might keep track of the different ways the hats can be placed. Suitable methods include drawings, linking cubes, squared paper to colour and using letter codes to identify each hat. Ask the children to work in pairs to organise and record their findings.

## Activity development
● When the children feel they have found all possibilities, gather their ideas and check to see if they have found them all (there are six).
● The following sequence is relevant here (although you should not expect children to grasp it in full):

| 1 item can only be placed 1 way | 1 |
| 2 items can be placed 2 ways | 2 × 1 |
| 3 items can be placed 6 ways | 3 × 2 × 1 |
| 4 items can be placed 24 ways | 4 × 3 × 2 × 1 |

● The children may, however, be introduced to the problem through discussion of object positions and choices. For example, with three hats you have a choice of three hats for position 1, a choice of two hats for position 2 (because you have filled position 1 already), and only one possibility for position 3 (because you have used the other two hats already).

## Review
● Compare the methods selected pairs used to record the possible combinations. Discuss and identify efficient methods.
● Can the children now say in how many ways the shopkeeper can display three shoes?

### Next steps
● Ask the children to predict in how many ways four hats could be displayed. Discuss how they might record their methods, bearing in mind that this question is more challenging than the three-hat task.

# Wizard hats

Three hats are sitting on a shelf in the Wizard accessories department of a shop. There is a star hat, a moon hat and a sun hat.

- ◀ In how many different ways can the hats be displayed? (You may like to cut out the pictures of the hats to help you explore.)
- ◀ Record your workings here.

Illustration © Gaynor Berry

# Packed lunch recycle

## Activity introduction

### Learning objectives
**(Y1) Data strand:** Answer a question by recording information in lists and tables; present outcomes using practical resources.
**(Y2) Data strand:** Use lists, tables and diagrams to sort objects; explain choices using appropriate language, including 'not'.
**(Y3) Data strand:** Answer a question by collecting, organising and interpreting data; use... pictograms and bar charts to represent results and illustrate observations.

### Expected prior knowledge
● Explain what recyclable objects are.
● Read information on a bar chart and pictogram.

### You will need
Adverts encouraging recycling and local authority publicity (optional); lunch box containing items with a variety of packaging (some recyclable and some not); centicubes or plastic linking cubes; interactive whiteboard (optional); photocopiable page 127 (one per child; alternatively, prepare five lunch boxes yourself or use the children's own lunch boxes); squared paper; coloured pens/pencils (optional).

### Key vocabulary
graph, representation, fraction of total

● Ask the children to talk about their understanding of recyclable materials, using some adverts encouraging recycling and local authority publicity to guide the discussion if you wish. Show them your prepared lunch box (see 'You will need', left) and discuss the contents, sorting what is recyclable from what is not.
● Show how you might represent this information using centicubes or plastic linking cubes (with one cube representing one item) and lay them alongside each other (alternatively, use representations of cubes on an interactive whiteboard). Discuss the type of graph you build. For example, this arrangement represents six recyclable items and three non-recyclable items:

● Hand out photocopiable page 127 (or, if using real lunch boxes, display them as appropriate). Working with a partner or within a small group, the children must decide which items are recyclable and which are not. The categorisation of each item must be justified and agreed by the group.
● Ask the children to construct a graph to present their findings (either using linking cubes or drawn on paper).

## Activity development

● Ask the children to discuss their findings. When you are happy that each pair or group has completed their graph and articulated their ideas, discuss the results as a whole group.
● If each group has a different set of lunch boxes to look at, you can then ask two groups to add their cubes together. This work can also be recorded on paper if you wish, although the practical element is the focus of this activity. You can then continue to combine results until you have all the cubes together, representing all the packed lunches.

## Review

● Review the totals achieved and ask appropriate questions. Talk about any difficulties or confusions the pairs/groups encountered, particularly when deciding what materials were or were not recyclable.

### Next steps
● Some supermarkets and department stores offer a child's packed lunch for purchase in their cafeterias. If possible, gather a selection of such lunches and present them to the children. The children have to decide which is the most recyclable packed lunch on offer in your local town. Afterwards you could present the information to the stores, together with the children's thoughts and ideas on the results.

# Packed lunch recycle

◼ Divide these lunch boxes into two categories: recyclable/non-recyclable packaging.

◼ What is recyclable?

_____

_____

◼ Use centicubes or linking cubes to represent your findings. For example, if there are seven items and three are recyclable, choose three cubes in one colour and four cubes of another and place them side by side on a piece of squared paper to build a graph (see example, right).

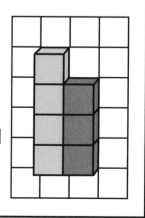

Illustration © Gaynor Berry